INTRODUCTORY.

DR. KARSTEN, a distinguished German botanist, was in New Granada for several years, and thoroughly examined the cinchona region of that country. His pamphlet, which has now been translated for the use of those who are entrusted with the cultivation of the cinchona plants in India and Ceylon, contains the results of his observations, especially with regard to the most favourable conditions of growth for the formation of quinine in circ

—ployed to collect seeds of the species of cinchonæ, yielding grey bark, in Huanuco, in 1860, which have since come up by hundreds, and produced healthy plants, both in the Neilgherry hills and in Ceylon.

Dr. Poëppig is the greatest modern authority on the cinchona plants of Huanuco, as Dr. Karsten is on those of New Granada.

CLEMENTS R. MARKHAM.

India Office,
    August 1861.

Poeppig, Eduard.-Reise in Chile, Peru,
und auf dem Amazonenstrome während
der jahre 1827-1832.   Notes on Chinchona trees in the forests of Huanuco and Huamalies.   This portion
trans. into English, with notes etc.

INTRODUCTORY.

DR. KARSTEN, a distinguished German botanist, was in New Granada for several years, and thoroughly examined the cinchona region of that country. His pamphlet, which has now been translated for the use of those who are entrusted with the cultivation of the cinchona plants in India and Ceylon, contains the results of his observations, especially with regard to the most favourable conditions of growth for the formation of quinine in cinchona plants. Many of his observations regarding the cinchonas of New Granada, will equally apply to the species found in other parts of South America.

The only valuable species in New Granada is the *C. Lancifolia*. Plants of this species, transmitted by Dr. Karsten, are now growing in Java; and it is possible that the Dutch Government may be induced to exchange some of them, for a like number of those species now growing in India, which yield the red and grey barks of commerce; and which the Dutch do not possess.

To Dr. Karsten's pamphlet has been added a translation of all that relates to cinchona plants, in the work of Dr. Poëppig. That eminent German naturalist and traveller thoroughly explored and carefully examined the cinchona region in the province of Huanuco in Peru, in the year 1830. His remarks will be a valuable addition to the report of Mr. Pritchett, who was employed to collect seeds of the species of cinchonæ, yielding grey bark, in Huanuco, in 1860, which have since come up by hundreds, and produced healthy plants, both in the Neilgherry hills and in Ceylon.

Dr. Poëppig is the greatest modern authority on the cinchona plants of Huanuco, as Dr. Karsten is on those of New Granada.

CLEMENTS R. MARKHAM.

India Office,
      August 1861.

THE MEDICINAL CINCHONA BARKS OF NEW GRANADA.

By H. KARSTEN.

HISTORICAL.

No subject in the study of pharmacy, is, probably, at present more complicated than the knowledge of the quina barks, which, with opium and ipecacuanha, belong to the most important vegetable medicines ; and just on this account it has found a great number of writers, who, unfortunately, are often unfitted to clear the dark places of a region unknown to themselves.

Attention was first drawn to the plants which yield quinine, on account of their fever-allaying bark ; and this happened before the botanists, pharmacists, and merchants distinguished and named the operative part, according to the difference of the exterior, or the place where it was taken from. Botanists first began to distinguish the different kinds of plants yielding the quina bark, and to decide as far as possible on the already known barks, at a later period.

After the magistrate, Juan Lopez de Canizares, had, in the year 1638, by means of a bark (*cascara* or *cascarilla*), of a Cinchona of the *Quinaquina de Uritusinga,* made known to him by an Indian of Loxa, cured the wife of the Viceroy of Peru, Don Jeronimo Fernandez de Cabrera Bobadilla y Mendoza, Conde de Chinchon, of intermittent fever; the properties of this excellent remedy became known in Peru, as also in Europe, through her, as well as through her confessors, the Jesuits, and her doctor Juan de Vega, under the name of *Polvos de la Condesa, Polvos de los Jesuitas* (*pulvis Comitissæ, Jesuiticus*); and Juan de Vega sold the first pound of quina bark, *Cascara de Quinaquina,* or *del Peru,* in 1640, in Spain, at 100 reals. The attention of botanists was first drawn to the mother plant of this valuable remedy, when in the year 1738 the learned astronomer, La Condamine, who, during his residence in tropical South America embraced and promoted every branch of natural science with equal love, gave his first botanical description of the *Quinaquina,* in the *Memories de l'Academie Parisienne,* 1738, *p.* 114, to which he added a drawing. Soon afterwards Joseph de Jussieu also examined the district round Loxa, and gathered, among other plants, the fever-dispelling Cascarilla, which, together with the observations supplied by Condamine, Linnæus made use of for the description of his *Cinchona officinalis,* in the first edition of his *Species Plantarum,* 1753, after he had already, in 1748, in the sixth edition of his *Systema Naturæ,* established the genus Cinchona, in honour of the countess of Chinchon, from whom the knowledge of the remedy in Europe chiefly proceeded.

Whilst the excellent effect of this remedy induced the Spanish ministry not only to commission the botanist Celestino Mutis, then in New Granada, (1760,) with the investigation of the bark of the Quina trees (*cascarilla o arboles de la Quina*), but also to send the botanists Ruiz and Pavon to Peru, in 1777, to study the Flora there, as well as to devote themselves to the study of the bark trees; the desire of gain was active on the other hand in concealing the place where these barks were found, and their derivation, for they had in the meantime been brought into trade, of various kinds and varieties, genuine and adulterated, mostly under the names of the harbours or towns of the continent which furnished them.

Unfortunately the vanity of the well-informed writers on the Peruvian bark, their envy of the discoveries of the industrious but little gifted Mutis, and the ignorance and frivolity of the scholars of the latter, have been the cause, since the commencement of the thorough study of the species and varieties of this very numerous genus (*Cinchona*

of Linnæus), of confusing the knowledge of it, and embarass-
ing their successors by erroneous synonyms.

After Ruiz had described seven kinds of Cinchonæ in his
Quinologia, edited in 1792, and Mutis his four kinds, observed
round Bogota since 1772, namely, the *Lancifolia, Cordifolia,
Oblongifolia*, and *Ovalifolia*, which he published in the *Papel
Periodico de Bogota*, 1793,* Ruiz added four more in his
Suplemento de la Quinologia, 1801, referring them to the *Cin-
chona* of Mutis, but declaring them to be entirely different
from the best Peruvian kinds (p. 26).

The very defective diagnoses of Mutis excuse, in some
measure, the error committed by the authors of the *Flora
Peruviana,* whilst still more inconsiderately, Zea (*Anales de
la Historia Natural de Madrid,* 1800) declared the species of
Ruiz to be varieties of the four Cinchonæ found near
Bogota.

As on the one hand the botanists unscrupulously and pur-
posely confused the knowledge of the species, the pharmacists,
on the other, allowed themselves to be misled into the
attempt to bring back the different fever-barks, prepared
under various names in trade, to the species imperfectly
known and badly described by the botanists, pre-supposing
that the bark of all *Cinchona* existed in trade. Now if this
was really the case at the beginning of this century, these
definitions, according to the descriptions of Ruiz alone, or
the commercial name of the barks (without at the same time
having a knowledge of the parent plant), could naturally
only turn out to be erroneous, and serve only to obscure the
knowledge of the subject in question still more.

The confusion in the nomenclature of quina barks was
increased through the altered commercial relations, caused by
the important discovery of Pelletier and Caventon, and also
through the erroneous statements of Ruiz and Pavon, who
had made the study of the *Cinchonæ* their especial task.
The works of Ruiz and Pavon were greatly wanting in per-
spicuity, as well as in system, from the double naming of many

---

* Compare Humboldt " *Magazin der Naturforschenden Freunde in Berlin,*
1807, p. 116, &c."

species; and in a pharmaceutical point of view from their fallacious statements as to the medicinal or commercial value of the barks of those sorts made known by them, which they estimated according to the success of the trade with them in Europe. Of the six sorts of Cinchonæ which they designated as particularly valuable for their bark, viz., *C. Micrantha, Glandulifera, Dichotoma, Lanceolata, Nitida,* and *Hirsuta,* only three deserve to be named as such, since only the *C. Lanceolata,* the *Nitida,* and *Hirsuta* yield a good alkaloid; whilst the *Micrantha* and *Glandulifera,* under the names Huanuco and Huamalies, certainly formerly yielded saleable barks, but their yield of quina is too small to be still valued:* the *C. Dichotoma* yields no medicinal quina bark, since it is no Cinchona, but belongs to an entirely different genus.

After the active crystallic element of the quina bark had been discovered by Pelletier and Caventon in 1820, the goodness of the bark gradually began to be determined according to the quantity of this element contained in it, and proceeding from the idea, that for every sort the contents of the bark in organic bases was constant, they made use of this circumstance for the classification of the barks, as well as for the determination of the parent plants. The barks without alkaloid were gradually excluded from trade by the manufacturers of quinine; but not so from the lists of the phamacists, who, on the contrary, thought they would increase the number of sorts, when they found a physically similar bark with a different quantity of alkaloid, such as the *Bogota, Pitayo, flava dura,* the different *Loxa barks,* &c. Likewise the specimens collected in the Herbariums, often only varieties of one and the same sort, frequently served the botanists as types of a new species; until in most recent times, when the generic characteristics of the Cinchona and its allies were revised by Klotzsch, the derivation of some barks was decided on by him at home, whilst those species growing in Peru and Bolivia were there examined and decided on by Weddell. After la Condamine and Humboldt had discovered the mother

---

* These two species yield a large per-centage of Cinchonine.—*C.R.M.*

plant of the genuine *Loxa Quina* to be the *C. Con-daminea, Humb.*, *Poeppig* showed that the *C. Glandulifera*, *R. et Pav*, and *C. Micrantha fl. per.* were the mother plants of the Huanuco and Lima barks. The derivation of the red bark is now known through Klotzsch, and that of the *Cinchona Calisaya* through Weddell, the first from the *C. Succirubra* growing on Chimborazo, the latter from the *C. Calisaya, Weddell*, both investigators having before them the parts of the plant necessary for their systematic determination, as well as the barks taken from them, whose usual name was known with certainty in trade.

When Weddell commenced his observations and researches on the *Cinchonæ* of Peru, he saw the barks of a small number of species only collected and sent into trade, and therefore received the commercial names of the greater number of his specimens of bark, which were used in former times, from Paris, through Guibourt. He did not examine the *Cinchonæ* growing in Columbia, and therefore did not know the barks which are there collected and exported.

He derives the red bark, which at the time of Weddell's residence in Peru, was no longer gathered, and which has now first been rightly determined by Klotzsch, with Guibourt (*Histoire des Drogues*, iii. 120), from the *C. Nitida, R. et P.* He, however, did not observe it living ; and from the description given of it by himself, as well as from the information given by Ruiz and Pavon, it is rather one similar to the Loxa Cinchona than the red bark. We must certainly agree with Ruiz, who considers that the species growing at Huanuco, Huamalies, Xauxa, Patanahuas, Moyobamba, Loxa, Jaen, Cuenca, &c., are very nearly related to the *C. Conda-minea*, as also the bark called by the natives *cascarilla fina*, and first gathered at Loxa.

Weddell did not examine the Cinchonæ growing in Columbia in their native place, and therefore he did not positively know the derivation of those quina barks exported from the districts formerly called Columbia, which already, at the end of the preceding century, were made known by Mutis, gathered at his instigation, and sent into European commerce.

Besides the four species known by Mutis, a number of others grow in New Granada, which he did not discover, but which are also mostly of subordinate interest in a medicinal point of view, as well as three of the kinds described by him : since the goodness of the bark is determined only according to its fever-curing property, *i.e.*, according to its content of quinine.

This content of quinine or other organic bases, generally varies very much in the different species of Cinchona, is entirely wanting in some, and corresponds in a remarkable manner with the form of the outward organs, particularly those which chiefly serve for systematic determination.

ORGANIC.

To the genus Cinchona of Linnæus, characterised by its author by the funnel-shaped corolla with hairy edges, and bivalved capsule opening from below upwards; he himself, and other botanists, added more species, whose capsules begin to open from the top, until Endlicher separated these, as a subordinate genus of the proper *Cinchona* of Linnæus ; and Klotzsch, combining the sub-genus *Cascarilla* of End-licher, with Buen Pohl's genus, characterised by the six-petaled corolla, raised them to an independent genus called *Ladenbergia.*

This systematic separation of the Cinchonæ of the older authors, into the genera *Cinchona* and *Ladenbergia*, corresponds very well with the existence of organic bases in their barks, since only the genuine Cinchona has hitherto yielded quinine, whilst the *Ladenbergia Moritziana, Kl. et Karst.*, and the *L. Macrocarpa, Kl.*, of Winkler, the *L. Riecheliana, Kl.* (*China rubra de Rio Janeiro Brasiliensis*), and the *L. Oblongifolia, Kl.* (*China nova, Ch. rubra de St. Fee*), have in vain been examined by me for this alkaloid. Mutis ascribes a soap-like taste to his *Quina Blanca.* Humboldt, who received this *Quina Blanca* from Mutis himself, remarks of it, that, kept in the mouth for some time, it produces an astringent and aromatic taste, and imparts its colour to the saliva.

I found no organic bases in the bark of the *C. Ovalifolia* (*L. Macrocarpa Kl.*), whilst Delondre and Bonchardat, *Quinologie, p.* 40, *plate* 22, in the bark described and represented, state, as the result of Henry's analysis, 6 *centigrams Chininum sulphuricum,* and 12 *centigrams Cinchoninum sulphuricum* in one kilogram. Judging from Delondre's very good representation, it cannot be assumed that Henry, like Mérat and Sens, examined a pale *Quina Flava Dura* for a true *Quina Blanca,* it is much more probable that, if the bark represented was examined by Henry, organic bases might also appear in the *Ladenbergia,* although not generally existing in it: in like manner the barks richest in alkaloids are, in some cases, found without these organic bases.

Delondre also states that the *Quina roja* of the *C. Oblongifolia* of Mutis, *Quinologie Mut.,* p. 41, contains cinchonine and quinine; but it will be perceived from his description and his drawing of the bark, that he erroneously takes a reddish variety of the *Quina Anaranjada, Mut.,* for it. The true *Quina roja, Mut.,* is that represented in Table 21, by Delondre as *Quinquina rouge brun,* in which no organic bases are found; and it seems to me not improbable that the bark represented on the same table, called *rouge pale,* and supposed to contain quinine and cinchonine, is the same plant, still covered with the outward bark, which I gathered in New Granada, in the province of Ocana, north of Bogota, at a height of 1,500 metres above the surface of the sea.

It may certainly be justly assumed that those Cinchonæ with the capsule opening from the base and crowned by the calyx, and having besides a corolla of delicate texture and bearded edges, and generally unindented seed lobes, give bark which can be considered pharmaco-dynamically as anteperiodic, whilst the species of the genus *Ladenbergia,* characterised by the capsule opening from the top, and mostly uncovered by the edge of the calyx, by perforated seed lobes, and by a generally large leather-like corolla with felt-like hairy edges, possess only astringent or tonic properties.

Not only from the specifically differently formed outward organs, can we judge of the absence or presence of quinine and cinchonine, but the proper medium quantity of those organic bases in the bark of the different genuine Cinchona-species can be nearly estimated from their form. The short, oval or elliptic capsules, crowned by the perforated or not perforated seed-lobe border, as well as the little scrobicules, which appear in the axillary vein, near the midrib of the relatively small leather-like leaves, are a sign of a regularly larger content of alkaloid in *this species;* whilst the large leaved unscrobiculate species, as well as those with long lance shaped capsules, or with porous perforated seed-lobe-borders, as in the *C.Purpurea, R. et Pav.,* the *C. Tucuyensis M.,* and the *C. Cordifolia, Mut.,* show a small quantity or total absence of quinine and cinchonine. These morphological relations to the contents of organic bases correspond at the same time with the relations of climate, which influence the developement of the different species, and their local extension.

GEOGRAPHICAL.

The scrobiculate leaved Cinchona, rich in alkaloids, inhabits the misty region of the Andes, where, in the nine months' rainy season, the constant rain is only interrupted in the day by interchanging sun rays and fog clouds, whilst in the season corresponding with winter, cold nights, in which the temperature sinks and the dark azure sky is lighted by the glittering brilliancy of innumerable stars, follow days in which the rays of the sun, warming the atmosphere to 24 degrees, now and then penetrate the thick fog which lies almost constantly on the damp foliage of the forest. The average temperature of this region is from 12° to 13° centigrade.[1]

The less healing, generally large leaved, unscrobiculate Cinchona, occupying a more extensive district, and living in some measure in common with the Ladenbergia genus, is more rarely refreshed by falling showers and rising fogs, in the dry season, when it has to bear a temperature rising to 36 degrees, whilst in winter it falls to 4–5 degrees of heat in

* 53° to 55° Fahrenheit. To convert degrees of Celsius to those of Fahrenheit, multiply by 9, divide by 4, and add 32.—*C.R.M.*

the morning, and the rain generally follows the sunny morning hours, from midday to midnight only. Whilst the former, *cascarilla fina,* is found the whole year with flowers and fruit, without any periodical change of vegetation, the latter, *cascarilla bobo,* colouring the border of the forest with the reddish shade of its dying leaves, is connected with the varying periods of vegetation.

The district round Loxa, whence we first obtained the healing bark, on account of its richness in species, might be termed the home of the Cinchona. It is also the centre point of the growth of this genus, which stretches from north to south for a breadth of 14 degrees, forming a narrow girdle to the plains of Columbia and Brasil, and covering the slopes of the plateau of the Andes, nearly from the foot of the Cordilleras, up to a height of 1,500 metres above the sea.

But the Cinchona with the small fruit, scrobiculate leaves, and rich in alkaloids, does not dwell in this horizontal expanse, but is confined to 11 degrees north and south of the centre point of their district of Loxa. It descends only to a height of 2,000 metres above the sea, from the cold summits of the mostly snow-capped mountains, where it sometimes reaches the upper limits of the growth of trees, *i. e.* 3,500 metres. Beyond these boundaries the proper Cinchona, *C. Australis, Wedd.,* occupies the southern outposts, and the *C. Tucuyensis, M.* and the *C. Cordifolia, Mut.* the northern, both without scrobicules in the leaves, and having large capsules, and too poor in alkaloids to furnish their bark for trade.

The genus *Ladenbergia,* which De Candolle joins with the Cinchona, on the other hand spreads in numerous species over the whole region of the South-American Continent lying between the tropics, from a height of 2,000 metres to 900 metres below, adorning the damp woody slopes of the warmer mountain zones with their large white fragrant blossoms.

· The *Exostemmas,* the *Remijias,* and most of the other plants belonging to the cinchonaceous order, partly inhabit the hottest regions of the tropical world, as far as the shores of the ocean: many species of them also formerly furnished their bark, under the name of quina. They are now, however, scarcely mentioned, e. g. the *Quina St. Luciæ* from the *Exostemma Floribundum L.*, the *China Nova* from *Lad. Oblongifolia m.* (Cinch. Mut.).

PHARMACEUTICAL.

In Columbia there are now only two essentially different kinds of quina bark gathered, the one discovered by Mutis at Bogota in 1772, whilst the other was discovered and tested for alkaloid by me a few years ago. Mutis, who discovered the above mentioned four species of Cinchonæ at Bogota, whose bark he distinguishes as *Anaranjada, Amarilla, Roja,* and *Blanca,* orange coloured, yellow, red, and white, declared the *Lancifolia,* whose bark is orange coloured, to be the especial febrifuge, at the same time holding it as identical with the *C. Officinalis, L.* (or *Condaminea, Humb.*) or the Loxa quina. He recommends it in intermittent fevers, whilst the yellow bark, whose parent plant he calls *Cordifolia,* is a strengthening remedy in remittent fevers. The red bark, from the *C. Oblongifolia,* he considered as an excellent *antisepticum* and *adstringens,* whilst he esteemed and recommended the white bark, especially in inflammatory as well as in continuing chronic and very obstinate intermittent fevers, as a dissolving and gently purging remedy. The two last species, however, belong to the genus *Ladenbergia, Kl.;* they contain no fever-dispelling alkaloid, and would do more harm than good in the cure of fever by their astringent properties; likewise the yellow bark of the *C. Cordifolia* is so poor in alkaloids that it cannot be used as an antiperiodic. These three species grow in the temperate zone, in regions which are partly inhabited and cultivated. They are, therefore, much more easy of access, and more convenient for profit than the *Cinchona Lancifolia,* which occurs in a rude rainy climate, dispersed in thick forests, far removed from human dwellings, and little visited, on mountain slopes divided by chasms and rushing torrents, where the sun seldom shines uninterruptedly for a few hours on the moist vegetation, where an open airy spot is scarcely to be found to dry the sap exuberant bark. The difficulty of obtaining the orange coloured bark of the *C. Lancifolia*, as well as the somewhat sanguine recommendation of the other barks by their discoverers, soon caused the particular estimation of the *Quina Anaranjada* to be forgotten by the collectors and traders. They were satisfied with the less healing, but, according to Mutis' statement, effective, and more easily obtained barks, which were chiefly, and soon only, shipped from Carthagena, Sta. Martha, and Maracaybo, brought down the Magdalena river to Europe, the one from the mountains of Merida and Trujillo, the other from the neighbourhood of Bogota, Pamplona, and Antiochia. Thus it happened that the Columbian barks soon fell entirely into discredit, especially since the quick and sure method of estimating their value, by Pelletier's and Caventon's discovery, was made known.

It is only now, in the most recent times, that this long abandoned branch of industry has been again resumed in New Granada. Dr. Santa Maria in Bogota, with the help of Cespedes, discovered afresh the *Quina Anaranjada* of Mutis, called *Tunita* by the natives, and lately it has been discovered in the whole Cordillera chain from Bogota to Popayan, shipped to Europe, and eagerly sought after by the druggists. But even now, since the cascarilleros have been taught by the European manufacturers that the *Quina Amarilla* of the *C. Cordifolia* is valueless, as likewise the red and the white barks of Mutis, and that only the *Tunita*, the *Quina Anaranjada*,* is of value in the preparation of the organic bases from which the quinine, cinchonine, and cinchonidine proceed : even now it has often been found that the genuine bark of the *C. Lancifolia* met with no buyers,

---

* Weddell and Bergen confound the derivation of the *quina flava dura* and *flava fibrosa*, which are only varieties of one species, with the *Quina amarilla*, Mut.; whilst Weddell places Bergen's *flava dura* with the *Quina amarilla*, Mut. (*Hard Carthagena bark*,) (*Quinquina de Carthagène jaune pale*), and calls Bergen's *China flava fibrosa*, *Quinquina de Maracaibo*, *Quinquina Cartagène jaune orange*.

because the usual quantity of alkaloid could not be obtained from it. The sellers thought themselves defrauded in Europe, and the buyers explained it by adulteration, or by a careless treatment of the bark; but even if both these facts be true now and then, the much more frequent cause is another, namely, *that in the same species of Cinchona the contents of alkaloids is not always the same.*

This I have found to be true, both in the *Cinchona Lancifolia, Mut.,* the bark of which on my arrival in New Granada was already peeled in many places near Bogota and Popayan, as also in the *C. Corymbosa,* a new species, similar to the *C. Hirsuta* of Ruiz, which I found between Tuquerres and Ibarra, on the western declivity of the volcanoes Cumbal and Chiles; from numerous analyses which I made on barks, mostly collected there by myself.

The *Cinchona Lancifolia* has a bark particularly rich in quinidine, yet its content of quinine amounts, on an average, to $2\frac{1}{2}$ per cent.; in rare cases it ascends to $4\frac{1}{2}$ per cent. of the sulphate, in others it appears more often down to 0. I gathered, on the different declivities of the volcano of Pasto, the bark of the *C. Lancifolia,* which seems here to have its most southern boundary, and I examined of the barks gathered from three places separately. One gave $\frac{3}{4}$ per cent., the second a slight trace of quinine, and the third showed no quinine whatever; the other crystallisable salts also were found only in slight quantity or not at all, and were not further examined. I obtained a very similar result from a dozen analyses which I made on different barks of the *C. Lancifolia, var. discolor,* gathered north of Pasto, in the forest of the district Tablon : some gave $1\frac{1}{2}$ per cent. sulphate of quinine, and a slight quantity of cinchonine, others 2 per cent. cinchonine without containing quinine, others no alkaloid at all, and the rest the same in various degrees, but none more than 1 per cent. quinine. These unexpected results could not be explained by the manner of investigation, for I examined them all according to the same method. The mistakes which might have occurred from the re-agents and imperfect vessels employed must have been repeated in each analysis, and therefore could not explain the various results.

I .always worked on the fresh undried bark, which was calculated at a third of its weight, since from repeated trials it had been shown that the fresh peeled bark dries up to a third of its weight; it was digested with sulphurated water (to each pound of moist bark 1½ drachms of sulphuric acid, and 4 pounds of water), until the decoction had no bitter taste, which was the case after three operations, then precipitated according to the known method with lime, the dried sediment distilled with alcohol, and by evaporating the same, after saturation of the organic bases by sulphuric acid, they were separated by crystallisation. In order to avoid the use of bone ash, which was difficult for me to prepare for want of an iron kettle, I crystallised the obtained alkaloids several times, and at last purified the sulphate of quinine, by dissolution in 40 parts boiling water, from the adhering cinchonine, quinidine, and colouring matter.

From the forest of Tablon three samples were gathered by a well-informed man, for the purpose of trade, from different parts of the same mountain ridge; the first only contained cinchonine 1½ per cent, the second no alkaloid, and the third very little quinine. All the barks were gathered from the lower stem, not of one tree, but one or more pieces of each tree, from a certain part of the forest searched, so that each analysis gave the average contents of alkaloid in the stems of that forest district.

Thus it is shown that the content of alkaloid does not depend on the individual differences of the plants, but that the soil or relations of climate, on which the nourishment of the plant depends, influences it.*

An exactly similar result, from an examination of the bark of the *C. Lancifolia* from Choachi, near Bogota, was communicated to me by Dr. Lazaro Santa Maria. The forest of a mountain ridge was divided into three parts, and the bark gathered from each separately, in a given manner. The

* This varying quantity of quinine and cinchonine, in the bark of the *C. Lancifolia*, reminds us of the variation, proved by several chemists, in the contents of *Morphium, Narcotin,* and the other alkaloids, in the juice of *Papaver Somniferum*, depending on the relations of climate under which this plant grew.

B

sample taken from one side gave $4\frac{1}{2}$ per cent. sulphate of quinine, the middle 2 per cent., and the last only insignificant traces of it. The nature of the soil showed no difference in all these cases. In the neighbourhood of Pasto it was the detritus of the Andes, near Bogota that of the chalk-clay-slate of which the declivities were composed; this variation, could therefore only proceed from the air currents coming from the summits of the mountains to the valleys, which are different on one declivity from another, and different again on the ridge, according to the sun or prevailing direction of the wind. As the snowy mountains of Sta. Martha, rising from the warm plain, and surrounded with the relatively dry sea air, are incapable of nourishing the genuine cinchona, although the temperature of the cinchona zone is not wanting in these mountains; so the *C. Lancifolia*, growing on the isolated volcano of Pasto, surrounded by the hot dry valleys of the Patia, approaches the species of its genus growing on warmer slopes, in respect to its contents of separatory matter; in like manner as the contents of sugar, starch-meal, and essential oil is dependent on the relations of climate, under which the plants grow, which secrete these matters.

In the analyses (communicated by Delondre and Bonchardat in the *Quinologie, p.* 33, &c.) of the Quinquina Calisaya de St. Fè, the *Q. jaune orange de Mutis*, *Q. Pitayo*, and *Q. rouge de Mutis*, the like variation of contents in organic bases in these barks occurs, by which Delondre and Bonchardat were led to conclude that they were distinct species of quina bark.

The observation of the *Cinchona Corymbosa*, on the western declivity of the volcanoes of Cumbal and Chiles, completely confirmed this opinion. Both volcanoes lie near each other, bounding the high plain of Tuquerres on the west; their eastern declivity is without trees, and grown over with grass and brambles, likewise the northern declivity of the Cumbal, which bounds the hot valley of the Guavo. The western declivity of both volcanoes is covered with thick forest, in which, in the upper regions, grows the *C. Corymbosa*. In the northern parts of the forest, bounding the Guavo valley, I found this cinchona particularly frequent, often in such large groups that they might almost be termed cinchona forests. Various analyses of the bark of this forest district showed, however, only ¾ per cent. of quinine, indeed, at the most northern limit of the forest, the stems, even in the highest parts, belonging to the district of Pipulquer, had no quinine.

The other trees also of this part of the forest, different species of *Rhopala, Codazzia, Weinmannia, Lettsomia, Clusia, Cletra, Sauranja, Ternströmia, Macrocnemum,* &c., indicated the proximity of the dry atmosphere of the Guava valley.

Those stems of the *Cinchona Corymbosa*, occurring in smaller number on the southward adjoining ridge, gave a bark containing 1¼ per cent. of quinine. This territory lies in the middle region of the vertical extent of circuit of this Cinchona; above, the forest growth was supplanted by grass which covered the very abrupt gravelly declivity, the lower part consisted of an inaccessible perpendicular rocky wall above a thousand feet high, bounding the east and western sides of the ridge, descending from the ice-covered summit of the volcano. The stems of the Cinchona, rooted on these trachyte walls, and discernible from the opposite heights, were therefore inaccessible for our investigation.

Another ridge, stretching from east to west, belonging to the volcano Chiles, and descending gradually from its summit, offered more favourable circumstances for observation. The trachyte stone was here heaped in layers, 100 feet high, one over the other. Here the brooks, springing from the ice of the mountain summit, had formed deep narrow beds, in which the trees of the forest, protected from the violent, icy, night winds, rose almost 2,000 feet above their upper limits, and stretched into the grass-covered plain. These ravines, widening towards the bottom, are the canals for the ascending air-current, when the mid-day sun warms the vegetation of the mountain slope. Here the fogs first form when the mists of the warmer atmosphere, rich in hydrogen gas, meet the colder air falling from the icy summit, and a frequently repeated change from thick fog, wetting the surface of the plants, to warm sun rays drying and warming the heavily dew laden leaves, continues until late in the afternoon, when clouds of mist spread over the whole region, until they are struck down by the night-cold, and resolved again into mist, by the later rays of the morning sun.

This is the proper climate of the Cinchona, rich in organic bases, so at least it is from my observations, for the bark of the Cinchona growing in the ravine described, high above the actual limits of the forest, gave 3½ per cent. sulphate of quinine ; whilst that from the lower lying forest taken from the *C. Corymbosa*, where the *Ladenbergia Macrocarpa* already appeared, scarcely yielded one per cent. This lower, luxuriantly vegetating part of the forest was situated in the region of the rain-clouds, where the colder mountain air falls into the stratum of the atmosphere, rising from warmer parts, and saturated with hydrogen gas ; and the mist constantly spread over the forest, and frequently changing to rain, admits the warming rays of the sun only in the summer. Then ascending to higher regions, the mist is almost driven away by the sun, and the periodical change of growth of the *Ladenbergia* here passes into the constant equal vegetation of the Cinchona, occupying the region of mist.

Similar differences in the atmospheric relations, produced by the air currents, often occur in brooks and ravines lying close together on the same mountain, according to their terminating higher or lower, with greater or less breadth, or in a woody or barren place. Often have I observed, in such a mountain ravine, the formation, continually renewed, of such mists, whilst in an adjoining but generally broader one, a constant sunshine rested on the vegetation : and no doubt similar circumstances cause the above-mentioned difference in the content of alkaloid in the *C. Lancifolia* grown on adjoining tracts.

Yet each species of Cinchona probably has its regular average content of alkaloid, which may amount in the *C. Lancifolia* to 2½ per cent. of quinine, and from 1 to 2 per cent. of cinchonine. If this average content of alkaloid could be exactly determined for every species of Cinchona, the plan of division for the quina barks, proposed by Plaff and Bergen, might perhaps be carried out. Since this regular relation, however, is subject to certain alterations from the change in the condition of the nourishing qualities of the climate, the principle seems impracticable. The age also of the plant comes into consideration, for the above quantity of quinine in the bark of the C. Lancifolia refers only to the bark of the full grown stem; that of the youngest branches has neither cinchonine (as Weddell thought he had found it in the *C. Calisaya*, in general so rich in cinchonine) nor any other crystalizable organic bodies in perceptible quantity. These are first found in the branches an inch thick, on which the cork is completely formed. The bark of the roots, at least the upper part, has its content, though in smaller quantity, of organic bases similar to those of the stem. In the anatomic structure this resembles that part of the bark of the stem, turned to the shade and wind.

The bark of felled stems, when it lies damp, remains a long time fresh and unchanged, and the content of quinine seems to alter only very gradually. I observed that one stem, whose bark at the time it was felled gave $3\frac{1}{2}$ per cent. sulphate of quinine, six months after had diminished only a half per cent., for which a crystalizing body was substituted, together with the sulphate of quinine from the alcoholic fluid, which crystalized into transparent gypsum-like concentrically grouped leaves, whose nature, however, could not be investigated, on account of the small quantity. The appearance of the bark of a stem of the *C. Corymbosa*, felled six months before, was completely that of a living tree. It covered the lower part of the stem, on the side touching the ground; the bark of the upper part of which had given $3\frac{1}{4}$ per cent.; the surfaces of the old cuts only were partially browned, otherwise, on turning the stem, the whole bark was found to be well preserved. After the peeling, as usual, during the first moments, it turned white and then brown, from the contact with the atmosphere. This oxidization of the tannic acid, taking place immediately it is exposed to the air, into quina red, and the consequent brown colouring of the fresh bark of the genuine Cinchona, does not take place in the above-mentioned *L. Macrocarpa*, Kl. From this reason Mutis named this plant *Quina Blanca*, an appellation which,

as it is according to nature, will be understood at once.
I observed this among the Indians (on my excursions in
the provinces of Pasto and Tuquerres, where these plants
were hitherto unknown) when they accompanied me in the
forests; that, after I had drawn their attention to the simi-
larity between the Macrocarpa and the true Cinchona, they
of their own accord gave the name *Cascarilla Blanca* to the
bark which they peeled for me. They, however, gave this
name also to a very different tree, namely, to a *Bignoniacea*,
with very bitter bark, the *Codazzia, Krst. et Triana*, which
grows in the same region as the *C. Macrocarpa*, because it
also turns dark very slowly, and is likewise bitter. Thus
every district has it *Quina blanca, amarilla,* and *roja,* without
its following that they are identical with the species fixed by
Mutis; and those who accuse Mutis of an error in the determination of his red bark, themselves make a great mistake
in wishing to determine the barks in trade, by the appella-
tions of the natives.

The remaining Cinchonæ examined by me in Venezuela
and New Granada, the *C. Cordifolia*, Mutis, the *C. Pubescens, C. Ovata* Ruiz, *C. Humboldtiana*, Lamb., as well as three
discovered by me, the *C. Tucuyensis, C. Pedunculata,* and *C.
Heterocarpa,* are not used for exportation. In former times,
as already said, the bark of the first-named species was exported, and the *C. Tucuyensis* furnished the *Ch. de Maracaybo.* Now, however, when the saleableness of quina bark
is determined by its contents of quinine, and the collectors
have learnt by experience that it is only the genuine unadulterated goods which cover the not inconsiderable expense
of collecting and exporting, these species, poor in organic
bases, are chiefly used as fuel.

Weddell states that, in Peru (Province of Caravaya), the
C. Ovata serves for the adulteration of the *Calisaya bark,* it
is also not much collected there, as little, as Pöppig informs
us, as the bark of the *C. Purpurea fl. per.* and the allied species
C. Cordifolia, Mut., and *C. Pubescens, Vahl,* in which last,
according to Weddell and Pelletier *Aricine* was discovered.

In the *C. Lancifolia,* various slight deviations occur in the size of the fruit and leaves, as well as in the form and hirsuteness of the latter. The capsule is generally 17 m. m. long, and 7 m. m. broad; it is sometimes narrower, sometimes longer, but the long shape always prevails. The lanceolate leaf, generally 12 centimeters long, in luxuriant shoots sometimes reaches the threefold length, some smaller varieties also which I examined, at 10 millimeters in length, approached the form of an egg, and on the under surface, with hirsute veins, were of a somewhat lighter green, almost blue-green, wherefore I distinguished them as a variety *discolor.** On account of the colour being something like that of olive leaves, this variety is called *hoja de Oliva* at Bogota. All these different forms, however, showed no *constant* alteration in the structure of the flowers and fruit, which could cause them to be considered other than mere variations of the *C. Lancifolia, Mut.* The leaves have little scrobicules on the under surface, in the corners of the veins, with hair round them, which appear on the upper surface, like small swellings of the cellular tissue of the leaf. These scrobicules, which are a general sign of the greater contents of alkaloid in the bark, have not been observed by most of the earlier investigators, and Weddell positively denies their existence, probably because he did not examine the living plant, and this peculiarity is more difficult to detect in the dried specimens.

Thus the quina bark collectors (cascarilleros) can be guided in the search for a good article of trade, by the form of the organs of a cinchona, and by the climate in which it to grows, yet for security it must be chemically analysed as to its absolute contents of alkaloid.

No practised cascarillero can hope to find a *cascarilla fina,* as the most effective medicinal cinchona is called, until the region of the *cascarilla bobo* (of the *C. Cordifolia,* &c., as well as the *Ladenbergian cascarilla blanca and roja*) is passed by ascending the declivity of the mountain; he may also

---

* This variety is distinguished from the species *discolor, Kl.*, growing in Bolivia, by the leaves, which are ovate-lanceolate ; in the *C. discolor, Kl.* they are subovate.

be guided by the small capsules, the small, hard, scrobiculed leaves, and the non-perforated seed lobes.

A cinchona, in general, may be distinguished from the other trees among which it grows (some *Lettsomia* and *Ternströmia* excepted), from the red colour of its dying leaves. This is the case also with the *C. Lancifolia*, which, in passing through the forest, where the crowns of the trees cannot be seen, is detected by the fallen red leaves, but not so when viewed from a height, for then the young leaves only are seen, and they may be recognised by the peculiar lustre of the smooth surface, even from a distance. This sign is less met with in the *Cinchona Corymbosa*, the leaves of which mostly fall without colouring, but the floral leaves always turn red before they fall. In the useless cinchonæ, the *Cordifolia*, *Pubescens*, *Purpurea*, *Tucuyensis*, and others, the colouring of the old leaves occurs much more strikingly than in the better species. Of the C. Lancifolia, the bark of which is characterised by the orange colour and by the yellow ochre, often pearly layer of cork, before it is peeled, the exterior sapless layers of cork, with the coating of Epiphytes, are scraped off. The cascarilleros do this with the large sabre shaped knife which they always carry with them, called *Machete*, and which they make use of to cut their way through the monocotyledonous plants. When they have arrived at a tree which they have seen from a distance, or suspected to be near from the red leaves, they scrape off the exterior surface of the bark, as far as they can reach; then, with a small chisel, they make incisions lengthways and across in the bark, so as to be able to strip it off in pieces 1 foot long and 1–2 inches broad. After having so far peeled the stem, they fell it with the axe, divide it according to the boughs, after having in like manner peeled the upper part. The smaller boughs and branches whose bark is too thin, they leave unpeeled in New Granada, because it is not very saleable in trade (like the Peruvian bark, through the prejudice of former times), and does not repay the bark peelers, who are paid for their labour, according to weight: the roots are left unpeeled for the same reason. Trees of the *C. Corymbosa* and *C. Lancifolia* are met with 60 feet

high, whose stems measure 5 feet in diameter: a single such
gigantic tree, which truly is not often seen, yields 10 cwt.
dried, or 30 cwt. wet bark; for which the bark peelers in
most places, receive about 3 dollars Prussian a cwt., if sold
fresh peeled in the forest and first dried, and furnished to
the nearest factory, they get 12 dollars per cwt.; the market
price in the towns is much higher. In Bogota and Popayan
the dry bark, at the time of my residence there, was paid for
at 30 dollars per cwt. The bark gathered round Popayan,
i. e. in *Pitayo* * and Purace on the Guanacas, in the southern
chain, as far as near Pasto, near Almaguer, &c., is exported
from Sabanilla, or Carthagena. The very bad roads and
difficulty of embarkation on the rapid flowing Dagua, as
far as Buenaventura, (for scarcely a boat passes without up-
setting, so that most of the bales of bark arrive in Buenaventura wet,) causes many dealers in Popayan to send their
goods the somewhat longer route by way of Honda and
Carthagena. Besides there are here many opportunities of
conveyance for smaller parcels, which do not offer in Buenaventura. The merchants in Popayan must therefore charter
whole ships, or at least the greatest part of them in Lima, in
order to induce the owners to send them to Buenaventura.
In order to avoid these evils, the quina dealers of Popayan,
as already said, rather choose the longer route, and either
send their bark over the Guanacas into the Magdalena valley,

---

* The name *Pitayo* has been confounded by some pharmacists, *e. g.* by
Batka, with *Piton*, by Kunze with *Pitoya*; and by the first and by Peretti the
Quina Pitaya with the *Quina Bicolorata* or *Atacamez*. Since the first sending
of bark from the *C. Lancifolia*, Mut., which general Mosquera sent from his
estates in Pitayo, in 1824, to London, through the consul general Henderson
in Bogota, in order to have it investigated as to its medicinal value, this
error seems to have been introduced by Bergen, who, in the "Magazine of
foreign literature for medical science, Hamburg 1825," refers to a communication of the "Times" of Sept. 24, in which mention is made of the consign-
ment of general Mosquera. Atacamez lies west of Ibarra on the western
declivity of the Cotocacha; thence came the *China Bicolorata*, which is probably derived from a *Pinkneya*, and still exists in collections of drugs: whilst
Pitayo lies on the western declivity of the Guanacas, near Popayan, and fur-
nishes an excellent *Quina flava dura*, from the *C. Lancifolia* growing there.
At the time when the forests of Pitayo were exhausted, the bark was sought
further and further in the adjoining forests, particularly in Totoro and Purace,
which furnish just as valuable bark, under the name Pitayo.

where it can be shipped at Neiva, and go by river down to Honda, where, on account of a low but long fall it is unloaded to be sent to Barranquilla, where it is stored until an opportunity occurs in the neighbouring harbour of Sabanilla to ship it; or the bales are shipped at Cauca to Carthago, where they are carried by beasts of burthen over the Quindiu pass, as impassable as the Guanacas, as far as Honda. At the time of my residence in those parts, the expense of the transport from Popayan to Honda, was 15 dollars for every cwt., and thence to Sabanilla, inclusive of export duty, about 10 dollars more. From this estimate of expense alone, it will be seen that bad quina barks would not pay, and since they almost all pass through the hands of manufacturers, only those barks containing at least $1\frac{1}{2}$ per cent. of quinine can be exported from Popayan.

The barks of the above-named large leaved Cinchona species, containing only a very slight quantity of alkaloid, are no longer demanded by the dealers; and as they do not grow together with the better kinds, but mostly in quite remote places, it would not be easy for the collectors to mix them secretly. Every intermediate dealer examines the bales before purchase, as to adulteration, which is easy to discover, for in almost all New Granada there is only one tolerably characterized good species; and it is well known from experience that in the transatlantic markets such adulterations only impede or completely hinder the sale. When, therefore, it is asserted by pharmacists, that in one bale of quina bark there are several different kinds packed together, I can with certainty deny that it is the bark exported from New Granada, in so far as different species are meant: and as to the Peruvian, I entertain great doubts, founded on the circumstances of its growth; for most probably each species has its especial station in the last-named place, as in Columbia, which it maintains unmixed with other species of the same genus. The bark of each species is therefore divided from the rest, collected and packed, and if the druggists in Europe pick out from one bale of bark *China Pseudo Loxa, Huamalies, Huanuco, &c.*, or *Pitayo Roja, Pitayo Anaranjada, flava dura, Carthagena*, &c., it is only a proof that these distinctions refer only to the outward appearance and variable physical conditions of the cork layer of the bark, which, in America, as in our European trees, naturally varies in one and the same species of plant, and it is an error to endeavour to trace these variations to a difference of species.

It is still easier to distinguish the genuine bark in the forests when fresh, for the colouring of the fresh peeled bark, from the oxydization of the tannic acid, offers a very characteristic sign for each, independent of the other physical properties. If one of the bark peelers attempted such deception he could be detected on the spot; therefore, it could only be from great neglect of the manager that such attempts would be made, and they would be discovered during the drying and packing.

As observed above, the Cinchona rich in organic bases, growing in the misty region, is found with blossom and fruit all the year round, now one tree now another, although the blossoming generally occurs in the dry season, which in Bolivia and Peru is from May to August, and in New Granada from November to March. The time of peeling the bark varies according to the manner of drying: this is generally done in New Granada by means of fire; wherefore people are occupied with the peeling and drying all the year, although during the violent rains it is difficult to induce the labourers to work, indeed it not unfrequently happens that this time is passed over, and the summer awaited. That this happens in order to gather the bark at the time of the ripening of the fruit, as stated by Ruiz and Pavon, " *Suplemento,* p. 41," is as incorrect as the opinion expressed that the old bark is almost useless, less healing than that of the younger boughs, and that the bark only of the middle part of the stem should be gathered. All these assertions were made *a priori,* serving as rules for the gathering of the bark of Caxanuma and Uritusinga, near Loxa, but this was only and solely to contradict the statements of Mutis. For, probable as the hypothesis of Ruiz may be, that with the different stages of development of the plant, the content of organic bases in the bark alters; yet experience tells us on the other hand that in certain forests bark cannot be peeled the whole year, and in others never. The drying in the sun is done only by smaller collectors, who dry the bark themselves, in order to take it to market or to the factories. The larger factories established in the forests, which take the bark fresh from the collectors, dry it by means of fire. It is impossible to do it otherwise in the forest itself, either in winter or summer. They would be obliged to pack it damp and send it to warmer places to be dried in the sun, and this could only be done in the dry season. In New Granada, where bark is peeled during the whole year, a kind of barn is erected in a part of the forest cleared for the purpose; *i.e.*, a roof of palm leaves, of the leaves of the *Heliconia*, or of grass supported by stems of trees, according as the warmer climate of the *cascarilla bobo* is farther or nearer the upper limits of the forest. In the region of the *cascarilla fina* there is no *Heliconia*, and seldom large leaved *Scitamineæ*, or palms, to which belong the *Geonome*. The large leaves of the *Anthuria* and *Philodendra*, which are laid five-fold for this purpose, rot too soon to be of service.

At a height of eight feet from the ground there are cross beams under the roof, on which a lattice work is made of palm-leaf stalks or bamboos. On this the bark is spread half a foot high; and a few feet under this lattice work, another is made for the same purpose; the supporting posts are also wainscoted with a similar open lattice, between which the thicker pieces of bark are put, and thus the walls are formed of quina bark.

On the ground of the hut, so constructed, several fires are lighted, and in their warmth the bark, which is turned from time to time, dries in three to four weeks. The drying must not be accomplished sooner than this, as the colour easily becomes too dark, and it is thought that the price may, in consequence, be lowered; whence it may be concluded that, from the greater warmth in the fresh moist bark, the organic bases decompose, of which I have made no experiment. The bark is known to be perfectly dry, by the edge, which is then yellow, whereas in the opposite case the middle layer retains the whitish yellow colour. The bark must not be placed too near the fire, as it may then take a reddish colour, or be blackened by the smoke. If removed too far from the fire it becomes mouldy, and is likewise refused in trade.

That the collection of bark is extirpating the Cinchona from its native land, as frequently said in Europe, is an unfounded supposition. From the base of the stem of the felled trees, when not deprived of their bark, a number of shoots spring out between the bark and wood, which truly would not occur if the bark were stripped off from the base to the roots, and also the ripe seeds which fall when the trees are felled, or before, germinate in the moist earth now warmed by the sun, and shoot up into a number of young plants, which, in the former thick shade, would not have had the necessary light for their development. The bark collectors, therefore, think that occupation increases rather than diminishes the number of trees. Truly in the forests searched, an interruption of 12 to 15 years takes place, as for instance at present in Pitayo and Loxa, but this only serves to promote the further investigation of the endless forests, and the discovery of ever fresh sources of this invaluable remedy, whilst in the mean time the young generation is growing up in the exhausted forests. A complete extirpation of the Cinchona can only occur, if, after the gathering of the bark the wood is completely cleared away and burned for the sake of agriculture, which relatively very rarely happens.

The dried bark (without separating the thin bark of the boughs, which is rolled up from the drying, from the stem bark, often half an inch thick), is packed in sacks of Manilla hemp (the bast of the leaves of the *Fourcroya*) in bales of 1 cwt. To facilitate the transport, the bark partly broken is pressed as tight as possible. In Bogota I saw the large fine pieces of bark spared as much as possible ; in Popayan they preferred pressing it, to reduce the size of the bales, as the purchasers in Europe are guided more by the contents of the quinine than by the outward appearance of the bark. The wholesale dealer wraps these sacks in bullocks' hides for their transport to Europe, the hairy side is turned inwards, and the bales are sewn in them, and the seam smeared with pitch.

As signs of the best bark of the *C. Lancifolia*, the *Tunita* of the people of Bogota, the following may serve : the orange colour of the inner bark, the yellowish glistening layer of cork, under which a dark brown line is often perceptible, the deep channel-like furrows from 1 to $1\frac{1}{2}$ lines broad, which are found here and there on the upper surface, and mark the scars of the fallen leaves, as well as the kind of cross fracture, which must be *short* and *finely splintered*, breaking almost like stiff card-board. The light-yellow layer of cork often forms excrescences and warts on the older barks. The bark of the lower part of the stem and of the roots, as well as that turned to the rain and wind, is more inclined to the formation of scabs than that which is exposed to the sun; the trough-like impressions form on it, which characterise the thicker Calisaya-bark. The thin bark is always rolled together, less purified from the yellowish cork layer than the thicker kinds, marked with faint irregular cross and long slits, all on the inner yellow-ochre coloured side, by the bast fibres, which are here closely pressed together.

The above mentioned variety with the ovate lanceolate leaves of the *C. Lancifolia*, which I have described as *discolor* in the forth-coming number of the *Flora Columbiana*, and drawn in *Table XII*, is distinguished by a more strongly indented cork and bark formation, on the stem by irregular slits, and deep trough-shaped excrescences of the cork into the bark, particularly on the lower part and the roots. The cross-section of the bast layer is very *short* and *fibrous*. The dark coloured layer, lying under the cork, consists of horizon-tally stretched, rarely cubic, thick-walled cells, filled with red-brown sap, giving a red appearance to the bark after the removal of the cork, whilst these parts are lac-red. It is these cells of colouring matter which communicate the orange colour to the exterior bark, in the *parenchyma* of which they are dispersed, and the inner part of which is yellow. Berg calls this kind *Quina Pitayo*, and distinguishes the intersected from the non-intersected bark as Buena-ventura and Sabadilla.

Another form, with smaller, less pointed leaves, which

I saw in the neighbourhood of Bogota, near Chiquinquira and Caquesa, but unfortunately had not the opportunity of sufficiently observing to determine whether it was, as I at first supposed, a variety *obtusata* of the *C. Lancifolia*, or an independent species,* gives a bark outwardly very similar to the genuine *C. Lancifolia*, but can immediately be distinguished by the long fibrous section, which proves it to be the *Ch. flava fibrosa* of commerce. This bark, as far as I have had opportunities of observing, contains always less, never more, than 1 per cent. quinine, and is therefore not sought in trade. The colour of the outward surface is the orange of the *C. Lancifolia*, or rather more red, sometimes also a yellow ochre with red spots. I have not examined the yellow *Ch. flava fibrosa* in trade.†

---

* The plant observed by me is distinguished from the *C. Lucumæfolia, Pav.*, to which it is no doubt allied, and likewise has truncated leaves, which, according to Lindley (Fl. Medicinal.) agrees with the *C. Stupea*, Pav., by the scrobicules in the axil of the leaf-nerve, which the *Lucumæfolia* does not possess, the specimens also given by Pavon as barks of the *C. Stupea* and *C. Lucumæfolia* are distinguished from that near Bogota by their red-grey-yellow colour, and thicker bast fibres, which are joined in rounder bunches; the section of the same is fine and brittle-fibrous, not so pliant-fibrous as the orange coloured bark, which I consider as a variety of the *C. Lancifolia*, and equally valuable with the *Ch. flava fibrosa*.

† Mutis, in his division into orange, yellow, white, and red quina barks of Bogota, made no distinction with respect to the kinds in the different localities. " He seems even to have designated this long-fibrous variety as " *Quina primitiva febrifuga*, and to have taken it for the best orange-coloured ; " for, according to v. Bergen, p. 297, the collection of barks lent to him by " Martius contained some which perfectly agree with the *Ch. flava fibrosa*, and " are termed *Calisaya de St. Fée*. According to Göbel and Kunze, " *Waaren-* " *kunde* i., p. 59," there was found in the collection of Frau Geheim-Räthin " Kohlrausch a packet of yellow *Ch. fl. fibrosa*, signed in Humboldt's own " hand : ' *Quina orangé de St. Fé, le meilleur de toutes les espèces connues* " ' *contre les maladies intermittentes. C'est le plus aromatique.*' A. v. Hum-" boldt received the bark from Mutis, and it was likewise sent to Ruiz by " Mutis, through Lopez, with the branches, as the typical form of the *C. Lan-* " *cifolia*, which Ruiz represented as *C. Angustifolia* in his *Quinologia*. Ruiz " describes this bark, sent to him by Mutis, as yellow in the fracture, ' *con* " ' *multitud de fibrillas longitudinales largas, agudas, muy delgados y desiguales*,' " (with a number of long, very thin, pointed and unequal small fibres); he " further compares it, evidently with the wish to say that all the Mutis " Cinchonæ are also found in Peru, with a bark gathered by Tafalla in the " damp hot woods of Chicoplaya, of a species similar to the *C. Lanceolata*, " which is, however, much more woody and of a darker colour, and in its " thick flakes with cast-off scales resembles much rather the *regia*.

Delondre and Bonchardat, in their Quinologie, describe two barks, p. 35 and 36, which are perhaps identical with the one observed by me. The first, called by them *Quinquina Carthagène ligneux* and represented in *pl. XIII*, which gives 2 per cent. of sulphate of quinine, they count among the best sorts preferred by the manufacturers. This statement, compared with my truly insufficient observations, perhaps corroborates that made above on the variation in the contents of quinine in one and the same kind of bark. The second, which they erroneously call Quinquina de Mutis, and represent in pl. XV, seems to belong to the same variety rather more red, wherefore it is called by the collectors *Quina carmin*. These chemists obtained from it 1·2 to 1·5 *Quininum Sulph.* and 0·6 to 0·7 *Cinchonin Sulph.*

The yellow bark of Mutis is derived, as already said, from the *C. Cordifolia, Mut.* (*Fl. Columb. Table VIII*), and is medicinally valueless, a coarsely cracked bark, cinnamon colour, yellow outside, covered with a glistening light yellow cork, which falls off later in irregular thick scales; thick-walled cubic resin cells are found in the outward bark, but not numerous; the bast fibre cells of the inner bark are of very unequal thickness, irregularly placed in rows, single, or a few in a small bunch, or joined in radial rows; the fibre cells next the bast-cells are likewise found with walls more or less thick. The sap-cells in the younger branches are not of long duration, and their outer bark dries in long wrinkles.

A yellow bark, formerly brought into trade as *Maracaibo Quina*, from the species *C. Tucuyensis m.* growing in the mountains of Merida (*Fl. Columb. Tab. IX.*) and allied to the *C. Purpurea fl. per.*, is now likewise no longer gathered; in Humucaro Alto, at the foot of the Paramo de las Rosas, I found packages of it piled up, which could no longer be sold. Outwardly it resembles the bark of the *C. Cordifolia*, with strong bark-scales, and almost cork-like, very short fibred in breaking; the bast cells stand more singly in the *parenchyma* web of the inner bark, surrounded by a few cylinder cells, which also sometimes become wood. The thick-walled resin cells are absent in the outer bark. Very frequently cells are found dispersed in the tissue of the bark, filled with small grains of oxalic-acid lime. Delondre and Bonchardat obtained from the *Quinquina Maracaibo* (*l. c. p.* 38, *pl. XVIII.*) 0·3 to 0·4 per cent. *Quininum Sulph.* and 1·0 per cent. *Cinchoninum Sulph.*

The bark of the *C. Corymbosa* m (compare *Fl. Columb. Tab. X.*) is grey, and resembles the Loxa barks: it is unequally finely splintered and fibrous in the fracture, more woody than that of the C. Lancifolia, inwardly of a grey cinnamon colour; outwardly, after the removal of the cork layer, of a dirty-yellow ochre. The surface of the younger branches, covered by the layer of cork, is of a grey colour, with fine and rather close transverse and irregular long cracks, these are sometimes so close as to give a scaly appearance to the bark, as the Pseudo Loxa is described. The older boughs and the stem have a thicker covering of cork, the cracks of which are farther apart, and out of which the *parenchyma* tissue of the cork bursts forth in warts and excrescences, like the Huamalies in trade, or the bark known as the *Ch. rubra suberosa.* Under the cork layer there is a darker layer, perceptible on the fracture, produced by greatly thickened resin cells. As above stated, I found most of these barks with very slight quantities of quinine, but in one place it was good, giving $1\frac{1}{2}$ per cent. sulphate of quinine, and in another it was excellent, giving $3\frac{1}{2}$ per cent. of this salt; on an average it might be equal to the Loxa or Huanuco. I cannot give a commercial name to this bark, as it had not yet come into trade, at least not from New Granada, where it was first gathered after I had drawn the attention of the inhabitants to it. Perhaps it will be called Tumaco or Barbacoas bark, because it is shipped from these places by way of Guayaquil, Buenaventura, or Lima to Europe. The packing is managed in various ways by the different dealers: some adopt the mode used in Popayan; others instead of bulls' hides take oil cloth; others pack it in bales of 1 cwt. in coarse flannel, and over that a coarse cotton cloth, both which stuffs are made by the Indians in Ecuador.

These commercial names and ways of packing however are of no interest, since the times are passed when these served for the distinction of bark. The pharmacists must prescribe the colour and contents in organic bases, and the druggists are obliged to test every sort of bark for its contents, since the colour and the derivation alone do not prove this.

All the bark of one plant, from the stem, boughs, and branches, is of the same ground colour. I very much doubt the statement of some pharmacists, that on one and the same tree there are grey, red, and yellow barks, or it must be said in reference to the spots on the surface, and not meant of the powder of the bark, or the exposed *parenchyma* of the dead cork, at least according to the rational description of colours. Even the youngest branches of the *C. Lancifolia* have the same peculiar yellow colour as the older barks : slight tints of colour also depend probably on the manner of drying, since the barks dried with fire soon take a reddish colour, whilst those exposed to the sun, and sometimes wetted by rain or dew, are more of a yellow ochre. The situation also no doubt in some degree alters the colour and relation of the elementary organs of the bark, as well as the form and consistence of the leaves, and their hirsuteness, as it likewise has a great influence on the development of the cork and the bark : still the ground tone of colour remains the same in each species, and the alterations in the anatomical structure never exceed the limits possible to each species of regular variation. To determine the latter, and to recognise the character of every species, would be the result of many comparative investigations.

ANATOMICAL.

GENERAL.

1. *Bast cells.* The barks of all Chichonæ thicken by the continual fresh formation of the bast layer out of the cambium, they are characterised by spindle-shaped, greatly thickened, relatively short bast cells, which in the inner bark, mixed with vertically extended cylinder cells, corresponding with the elementary constituent parts of the wood, are placed in radial rows, divided by lines of pith cells, which is caused

by the continued vegetation of the tropics. In the species of
the genus Cinchona the bast-fibre cells, which at first contain a
brown sap, in which little bubbles and grains are swimming,
are later thickened to a degree, so as almost to close the cavity
of the cells, the thickening layer of the daughter cells is interrupted by a few fine porous canals, and only the youngest
bast cells, lying nearest the cambium, have a cavity. In the
species of the genus *Ladenbergia,* these fibre cells are indeed
thickened, but still have a more or less considerable lumen
(Tab. ii, 17 & 18); those of the first species are much thicker
and shorter than those of the last, which also have much more
considerable porous canals. The cylindrical, mostly thin-
walled cells, which, with the rays of pith, form the changing
tissue into radial layers, in which the bast cells appear, more
or less numerous and differently grouped, are likewise formed
with a more or less thickened coating of their concentrical
skin, in every stage of transition, from the above cylinder-
cells to proper bast-cells. Since the rays of pith in the wood,
as well as in their peripheric continuation in the bark, sometimes extend in vertical space; *i.e.,* instead of consisting of a
single layer of cells, they consist of three and four layers,
which appear on the periphery in the form of an ellipsis,
so that the next standing vertically stretched spindle-
shaped and cylindrical cells of the inner bark are mostly
bent in the form of a bow, the rest lying close to them
approaching the normal shape; the whole tissue in the tan-
gential section thus obtains a net-like appearance from
these variable extensions of the pith rays. From the same
reason broader and narrower pith rays are seen in the cross
section of the bark.

2. *Sap fibres.* The primary bark *parenchyma* of all Cinchonæ, in the youngest branches, is divided by a circle of
cells, which contain the quina tannic acid mostly in a brown
red gum-resinous sap, generally stretched lengthways and
placed in vertical rows one above another, and which in many
species blend into continued fibres, from the cambial tissue,
in which, within the peripheric portion, the bast cells are
formed during the thickening of the wood cells on the cen-

tral side. It appears that no species of the genus Cinchona of Linnæus is devoid of these sap-holders * in the bark of the youngest branches. In the Ladenbergia they are particularly wide and joined to fibres so called milk-sap-vessels. In the Cinchonæ they are generally narrower, often not joined to fibres, and in many species soon entirely wither, so that in branches two years old and older they are no longer to be discovered. In the pith tissue these elementary organs likewise exist near the partition, they are more numerous and larger near the leaf knots than in the midst of the internodules. In general it may be said that in the medicinally efficacious species with smaller, harder, dimpled leaves, these sap vessels are more imperfect than in the large leaved dimple-less species resembling the Ladenbergia: but this is not without exception, since, for instance, in the bark of the *C. Glandulifera*, R. et Pav., which takes a middle place with respect to its medicinal value, and has small dimples in the angles of the veins on the under surface of the leaves, there are considerably wider sap-holders also in the older branches, until they are thrown off by the formation of bark in the adjoining tissue; of the two red barks, which both belong to the richest in organic bases, the one which, according to the statements of Delondre and Bonchardat, gives 1·5 to 1·8 per cent. quininum sulphuricum, and called by them rouge pâle, has wide sap-fibres, whilst the other, from which these chemists obtained 2·0 to 2·5 per cent. quininum sulphuricum, and called by them rouge vive, discovered none of these elementary organs.

3. *Resin cells.* The originally spherical cells of the primary bark, which is later separated as outer bark, by the sap-cells or fibres, from the inner bark containing the bast-cells, are horizontally placed and in lieu of the bast-fibres, these cells single, or several together forming groups or layers, are found with strong porous thick walls, and filled with a resinous

---

* Perhaps with the exception only of the *C. Hirsuta*, Ruiz et Pav.

fluid, very like that contained in the sap-vessels. The thick walled bast-cells are found, as already said, more perfect in the inner bark of the Cinchona, and of a more regular thickness than in the Ladenbergia, whereas these porous thick cells of the outer bark are much more strongly developed in the species of the latter genus than in the genuine Cinchona. In some of the Ladenbergiæ e. g. the *macrocarpa* (Cinchona Vahl), they form almost complete layers within the cork, alternately with slight layers of parenchymatic cells ; besides this, in the species of this genus, the bast-fibres of the inner bark are also vertically placed and joined in bunches like those of the Cinchona ;* whilst in these and on an average in the medicinally more efficacious sorts these resin cells seldom appear or are entirely absent, e. g. the red barks, in the Calisaya very seldom, in others more frequently, never in so perfect a degree as in the Ladenbergia. No general rule, however, can be drawn from the circumstance of the appearance of these resin cells, for in the medicinal kinds also they often appear in large numbers, e. g. just in our orange coloured bark, where they form the dark line under the cork on the fracture. These elementary organs of the outer bark standing in connection with the cork and the bark, after they have been thrown off by the formation of the bark, form also in the increased *parenchyma* of the inner bark between the bast-cells, with which they likewise blend later ; they are therefore in tissues in which the organic bases probably disappear simultaneously with their appearance.

The other horizontally placed, not thickened bark-cells near the cork layer also become filled, in some species and in certain places, with a similar dark coloured sap, whereby on the surface of the fracture of the dried bark a shining dark layer becomes visible, the so called resin-ring, whose existence or absence has served for the division of the

---

* These vertically placed resin-cells are often somewhat like the thick short bast-cells of the good quina-bark, but are immediately distinguished by the larger lumen of the cell, and the larger porous canals of the walls.

quina-barks, particularly of the Peruvian grey barks. But as this richness of resin occurs only in older barks, and as it appears in certain situations, the division founded hereon does not always agree with the derivation of the barks, although this circumstance may serve as an indication. After the casting off of the outer bark by the formation of the bark, the above thick-walled cells are found also in the increased *parenchyma* of the inner bark between the bast-cells.

4. *Lime cells.*—Some cells of the inner as of the outer bark and of the pith, particularly in the younger tissues containing starch-meal, are filled with small grains of oxalate of lime, the appearance of which, however, does not seem to be constant, perhaps, as with the appearance of the organic bases, it alters with the change of the nourishing properties.* They appear in the genuine Cinchona, as in the Ladenbergia, more seldom however in the first, and less in the hard- than in the soft-leaved sorts, a sign of inferior quality therefore. They are very numerous in the Ch. Maracaibo of the *C. Tucuyensis m.*, and in the Ch. Cusco of the *C. purpurea fl. per.*, according to Howard.

5. *Cork* and *bark.*—The outer crust of all Cinchonæ disappears as the bark forms, and even the bast layer of the inner rind is changed on the outside into bark, and on the inner side it grows afresh. In the different species of Cinchona the bark is formed in very different ways, depending on the situation ; in some the parenchymatic-cork is formed; in others the sponge-cork, consisting of radiated rows of cells ; in others again the cork consisting of table-shaped cells, the periderma or flake-cork, prevails, which last, when it pierces the tissue of the rind or of the sponge-cork, forms

---

* The growth of the cells containing oxalate of lime is generally slower than that of the adjoining tissue, so that their walls remain thinner, and even in the full grown tissue the globular cells may be seen within the mother cells lying from two to four one over the other in a vertical position; whilst the equally large adjoining cells have their walls pressed together, and appear in the usual polyhedrous form, which many anatomists now consider as arising from simple partitions.

the so-called bark-scales.* The form of the cork and bark
formations gives an excellent and very striking indication for
many species of Cinchona, which depend particularly on the
conditions of climate for their perfection; for instance, for
that growing on sunny, grassy declivities of the Andes of Peru,
freely or among the low shrubs, the *C. Bonplandiana*, Kl.
allied to the *C. Condaminea*, Humb., and for the *C. Calisaya*,
Weddell, which, according to the observations of this botanist,
in the valleys of the temperate zone of Bolivia, descends to a
height of 5,000 feet, towering above all the neighbouring

---

* Already in very young branches there is often found, directly under the
epidermis, a not inconsiderable layer of the table-shaped periderm-cells of the
flaked-cork, forming a close mantle round the inner cell-tissue, furnishing the
same with the elements of the atmosphere necessary for its nourishment, and
preventing the evaporation of the fluid which moistens it. In rather older
branches the layer of this flaked-cork is found much increased, and not only
by the increase of this originally existing layer of cells proceeding from the
cork-cambium, but by the direct transformation of the bark-*parenchyma* into
these radially placed cork-cells. The thin-walled, round, polyhedrons or cylindrical cells as well as the thick-walled resin- and bast-cells, all change their
original functions, become filled (whilst the former thickened coating, the
so-called thickening layer of the mother and the daughter cells is resolved)
with a dark fluid, which, as the transformation into the radiated cork-cells
approaches, becomes lighter, and join themselves partly directly partly after the
formation of new cells, inwardly to the cork, in order sooner or later to serve
as cork-cambium, that is, as mother-cells of cork-cells. The nature of the
cork and the composition of the bark vary according to the different stages of
development predominating in the cork-tissue. The bark of the Cinchona does
not consist of parallel layers of the different bark tissues, but, as in the plantain,
the cambial action seizes some of the trough-shaped layers of the bark-tissue
more or less prepared for the formation of flaked-cork, the edges of which
are connected with the peripheric cork-layer, and enclose groups of that rind-
or, bark-tissue, which is thereby withdrawn from the flow of sap, and without
reaching its destination dries up, without having served to increase the cork-
tissue. If the outer crust is thus entirely transformed, a similar course of
development takes place in the inner bark; the cells of the pith-rays, the
fibre and bast cells, all change their functions, the last latest, whilst their
walls are resolved in the same manner as the thick-walled resin-cells. This
resorption is frequently not completed in all these, and they are found in
their original form and constitution enclosed in the flake- or sponge-cork, or in
the bark-tissue.

These different stages of development of the cork, as metamorphoses of the
perfected bark-tissue, have not yet been described in the two excellent works,
which we possess, on the form of the bark and cork by Mohl and Hanstein.

trees of the forest. For this species, surrounded frequently by a dry atmosphere, moistened by passing mists, an often repeated formation of the flake-bark seems a rule, caused by the change of the drying and cracking of the outer bark-and cork-layer, and the moistening and springing up of the *parenchyma* exposed at the bottom, which is immediately changed into cork tissue, as the cicatrisation of the wound. If the cracked cork-tissue be removed, the cicatrised cracks are perceived on the surface below as flat furrows. The *C. Lancifolia,* growing in the constant damp atmosphere of the mist region, is on the contrary characterised by a stronger formation of parenchymatic-cork, and irregular cracks and excrescences of the flake-cork. I have mentioned that I have observed both kinds of bark formation in the C. Corymbosa, in the damp shady thickets of the forest, the cork formation on the lower branches and stem, whilst the smaller trees on dryer soil on the border of the forest repeated the bark formation of the Calisaya and Condaminea.

This dependance of the bark development on the climate renders the recognition and characterization of the bark of many of the Cinchonæ very difficult; yet with many, a good indication is the trough-shaped scales of the *C. Calisaya,* Weddell, and *C. Lanceolata,* R. et Pav., the cork excrescences for the bark of the *C. Micrantha,* for that of the stem of the *C. Corymbosa,* and of the *Ch. rubra suberosa,* which is, perhaps, only a variation of the *Ch. rubra dura* grown in a damper climate, at the same time corresponding with the statement of Poëppig concerning the colour of the bark of the *C. Glandulifera,* that the same is lighter in warmer regions, so that, perhaps, the light *Ch. rubra dura* proceeds from the same species in a warmer climate, which in a cooler moister one yields the dark *rubra suberosa.* This supposition also finds a ground herein, that Pavon terms the bark-rind (*Ch. rubra dura*) *C. Succirubra* in his bark collection, whilst, according to the verbal communication of Hr. Klotzsch, which will soon be more fully detailed by him, and published in the "Transactions of the Berlin Academy," in Pavon's Herbarium, a species is designated as *C. Succirubra,* from.

which, according to recent observations on the west declivity of the Chimborazo, the *Ch. rubra suberosa* is gathered.*

The mostly irregular cracked bark of the *C. Lancifolia* consists chiefly of proper bark *parenchyma* (the lowest stage of development of the cork from the bark *parenchyma*), whilst all barks now known in trade as Loxa, Pseudoloxa, and Huanuco, are covered with a perfect cork tissue.

ESPECIAL.

The fibres of the inner bark, whose position is so characteristic of the Cinchonæ, and whose form and coating is more proper than any other sign for the distinction of a true *Cinchona* from a *Ladenbergia*, also furnish a useful mark for the distinction of single species of the genus *Cinchona*, together with its other anatomical relations and its physical relations.

The more or less perfect and uniform thickness of the bast cells already shows the contents in organic bases; the good red and yellow barks are mostly easy to distinguish by the complete filling up of the cell spaces, from the grey Loxa barks.

In the younger branches the radiated layers of pith cells extend themselves in the bark tissue by a cross extension of their cells, in such a manner as to attach the outer bark, and thus form wedges narrowing to the centre, where they continue in the pith-rays of the wood, inclosing wedges

---

* If this hypothesis be confirmed, the *C. Succirubra*, Pav. would at the same time furnish a proof that the function of the sap fibres must be more necessary to and of longer duration in the individual of the varying dry warm region than of the moist and temperate climate, which I have hitherto not observed in *one* species of plant; it agrees however very well with the organic relations of plants in general, since those plants provided with more active gum- and resin-fibres generally have an intermitting character of vegetation, either caused by decay, as in the *Cycadæ, Ficoidæ, Umbelliferæ, Terebiuthaceæ, Clusiaceæ, Euphorbiaceæ, Legumini*, &c., or by changing cold weather, as in the *Coniferæ*, In the temperate moist climate of the cooler mountain forests of the equatorial regions resin- or gum-yielding plants are relatively rare, *e. g.* some species of tree ferns, Aroides, Lobelias, Clusia, &c.

of the tissue of the inner bark, corresponding to the woody fibre tissue, against which they lie with their broad sides, and sharpening towards the periphery. In these points or borders of the wedge of the inner bark formed of cylindrical cells* the Bast fibres generally lie singly dispersed, even when they are joined several together in radiated rows, or bunches inclining inwards towards the wood, especially in older barks ; and in a few species bunches and radiated rows of bast cells are found already in these outer borders of the inner bark, which then in older parts increase in the number of single bast-cells, and become thicker. On this order of the bast-cells, whether they stand singly, in radiated rows or bunches near each other, whether these bunches hang in a vertical direction to each other or lie singly in the unthickened cell-tissue, the transverse fracture of the bark depends, its being fine or coarse-splintered, long or short-fibred, properties which are of particular importance in the determination of the medicinal value, consequently also for the investigation of the sorts of bark, even though the species which yields it cannot thereby be recognized, since the C. Lancifolia shows us that these circumstances also change in the barks of the different variations of one species.

In the older barks several bast cells generally stand close together, even in those cases where they are placed singly only in the younger bark. In the genuine red barks, in the *C. Calisaya*, the *C. Lancifolia* var. *discolor*, the *C. Tucuyensis*, and in most, the bast cells are found on the contrary almost single in the older barks, although placed in rows yet divided by one or several not thickened cells. In the Uritusinga de Loxa, which appeared in trade during the first periods of the employment of Quina bark, as King's bark instead of Calisaya,* the relatively thin bast

---

* The Spanish Creoles still have the custom of giving the name *real* or *del rey* to the best, most beautiful, and most valued articles; thus every place has its *Palma real, Quina del rey*, &c. Whether the Uritusinga bark is really not from the C. Condaminea, Hmb., but from another hitherto unknown species, which Pavon named C. Uritusinga, later travellers will decide. That nearly allied to the C. Condaminea, the C. Bonplandiana, Kl., has much thicker bast cells even in the thinnest barks.

cells stand close together in radiated rows, therefore it is very easy to distinguish it from the present King's Quina of the Calisaya. The bark of the C. Lancifolia, Mut. also belongs to this category ; as in the Uritusinga bark of the C. Condaminea the sap-fibres disappear already in the boughs three years old, not indeed in consequence of the formation of the bark, which occurs later, but in proportion to the extension of the bark cells they contract and at last become imperceptible, because, as I have several times re-marked, new cells form in their cavity, similar to the parenchyma cells; the bast-fibre cells appear in the young branches at first singly, later however they range themselves in the different varieties or variations of this species in very different ways, sometimes in radiated rows standing alone, some-times in several single or double rows close together. So it is with the size and thickness of the bast-cells, which in one sort are like those of the Calisaya, and in the other like those of the Uritusinga;* in others they are of different sizes without order, or mixed together in kinds of layers, forming therefore in the cross section of the stem concentrical circles which, although imperfect, remind us of the arrangement of the bast of those plants which live in temperate or cold climates with a periodical change of vegetation, which was the case in the specimen of the C. Pubescens examined by Weddell, (Hist. Nat. des Quinq. Tab. 11, Fig. 31), and he held it as the typical order for the bark-bast of this species. A bark of the C. Pubescens, Vahl, examined by me, and which I found near Gacheta in the neigh-bourhood of Bogota, in a damp forest, somewhat below the region of the C. Lancifolia, showed quite a different arrange-ment of the bast-cells; here they stood neither so closely pressed together, nor in concentrical layers round the axis of the tree, but in radiated rows, and indeed very singly, in the parenchyma of the inner bark; yet I doubt not but that the

---

* It is interesting to know that the variety of the C. Lancifolia richest in organic bases has also the thickest cells; whilst the variety discolor, which in many places is so poor in quinine that it is not gathered, has the thinnest bast cells of all the C. Lancifoliæ.

order of the bast cells observed by Weddell may occur in the same species of plants.

The *C. Pubescens* does not like the damp misty region of the primitive forest of the temperate mountain zone, in which I gathered the bark examined, but the sunny borders of the forest, and the grassy declivities of the cloud-region above described, where, like the *C. Cordifolia, Ovata, Tucuyensis, Purpurea*, and similar ones, it may probably be subject to periodic growth, from the protracted dryness of the summer, which is shown in the bark by the changing bast and *parenchyma*-layers, and by the bast circles parallel with the surface of the stem.* On the other hand, if a species of plant of periodic growth reaches its upper limits, or in some cases oversteps it into a higher region with a less variable climate, it is probable that according to the nature of its development, the order of the concentrical layers, corresponding with the progressive growth, will change into radiated rows. I consider this explanation of the deviation of the statement of Weddell, from my observations on the structure of the bark of the *C. Pubescens*, the more justified, as I observed the same in the young bark of a bough three years old, of the *C. Lancifolia*, in which, on the sunny side, the bast-cells were almost in concentrically arranged layers, and on the opposite side were placed in radiated rows: in the older parts of the stem the concentrical order was lost, probably because in the deeper layers of the tissue, covered with the layer of cork and moss, and untouched by important changes of climate, a more equal development and unfolding of the elementary organs took place.

I take the same explanation for a bark, which, on almost the most northern limits of the *C. Lancifolia*, in the neighbourhood of Chiquinquira, is yielded by a truncated-leaved variety of the same, which I have designated as var. obtusifolia, very like that known in trade by the name Quina flava fibrosa (represented in v. Bagen's table iv, fig. 7-11),

---

* I observed a similar but opposite circumstance in the wood of the *Sambucus nigra*, which, grown in such a temperate Cinchona climate, had no *year rings*.

in which the radiated and often double rows of bast-cells project over the cell tissue in the transverse fracture, as long pliant fibres. This is distinguished from the yellow Ch. flava fibrosa in trade, by its more reddish orange colour; it most probably, however, belongs to the same species. In this bark thinner and thicker bast-cells are found more or less regularly placed in varying concentrical layers, similar to the year rings of the wood which are also found in those Cinchonæ growing in a periodically changing climate. This bark likewise gives a proof, that the thickness of the bast-cells is no deceptive sign of the greater contents in organic bases; although in general this is of some importance in the determination of the goodness of the bark, especially when the strength and manner of thickening of the walls are taken into cônsideration. In this variety also the porous canals of the thickened walls are rather wider than in the sorts richer in quinine.

The bark of the *C. Lancifolia* richest in quinine, which can scarcely be distinguished from the typical form called *C. Angustifolia* by Ruiz, except by the somewhat smaller leaves, and by the dealers of New Granada Calisaya of all variations or varieties of the *C. Lancifolia,* has the thickest bast-cells, almost to the disappearance of the lumen, which in this variation also deviate most from the regular radiated order. Delondre and Bonchardat obtained from it 1·0 to 3·2 per cent. quinin. sulph. and 0·3 to 0·5 cinchonin. sulph.

In that *C. Lancifolia* observed near Bogota, and mentioned above, whose bark partly gave 4½ per cent. quinine, the bast-cells are, on the contrary, most regularly placed in rows; therein similar to the true *C. Calisaya,* Wedd., that they do not stand close together, but are divided by single unthickened cells. It is, however, immediately distinguishable from the proper Calisaya by the great number of thickened resin-cells in the outer bark.

In the broad-leaved variety which I designated as *discolor,* from the forests of Pasto, and which I analyzed several times as described above, the relatively thin bast-cells stand rather singly, sometimes quite isolated, sometimes in twos, more rarely in threes, in the relatively large celled *parenchyma.* In this bark the parenchymatic cork-tissue, designated above as bark-tissue, is generally very perfect, and correspondingly so the cell-tissue of all the pith rays, which intersect the tissue of the inner bark, as well as the body of the wood, and widen considerably towards the outer bark.* The Quinquina Pitayo, of Delondre and Bonchardat, (l. c. pl. 12), seems the same bark; they obtained from it 2·0 to 2·5 per cent. quininum sulph., and 1·0 to 1·2 per cent. cinchonin. sulph.

The form of the *C. Lancifolia* drawn first by Ruiz, which he named *Angustifolia* (*Quinologia, Suplemento,* p. 10), with respect to the order of the bast-cells stands in the middle of these variations, in so far as these cells are placed in rows, sometimes single, sometimes several close together, more rarely two rows joined in a radial bunch, now and then also in round bunches.

To these yellow barks of New Granada are joined, with respect to the colour of the bark-*parenchyma,* as well as the size and position of the bast-cells, the *Calisaya,* from Bolivia, made known to us by Weddell (*Hist. Nat des Quinq. Tab. xxviii Fig.* 1), according to v. Bergen, known in Dutch commerce since 1790, as *Quina Regia;* it is also enumerated among the yellow sorts. It is, however, always more cinnamon colour, or rusty yellow, not so orange-coloured falling into yellow ochre, as the anaranjada of New Granada, which, from the repeated formation of periderm-layers of strong bark scales, are here mostly more regularly quadratically intersected, than is generally the case in the former, and is hereby distinguished from most other barks. The thick-walled porous resin-cells, so frequent in the bark of the *C. Lancifolia,* are very rare in the Calisaya. The sap fibres are retained in this species somewhat longer than in the C.

---

* Seeds of this variety, containing 2 per cent. quinine in the bark, I gathered in order to send them, through Herr v. Landsberge, Governor of Curaçoa, to the Dutch government, for plantation in Java. These were sown by Dr. Hasskarl, and have thriven excellently in their new situation. The result of this plantation will be interesting, in a systematic, as well as especially in a pharmacological point of view; we shall probably, in due time, receive information of it from the Dutch government.

Lancifolia, although they also here soon change their original function. Weddell distinguishes in the yellow *Calisaya* a white, gold-yellow, and orange sort. The thick flat barks of the first are distinguished by the trough-shaped impressions on the outer surface cleared of bark, the scars of the bark scales; whilst in the latter these scales do not separate from the inner bark leaving impressions, but quite flat from the surface, as in the *C. Lancifolia.* Delondre and Bonchardat represent the first, (*Quinologie, Tab. I.,*) and state that they obtained from the thick flakes 3·0 to 3·2 per cent. quinin. sulph., and 0·5 to 0·8 per cent. cinchonin. sulph.; from the thinner rolls 1·5 to 2·0 per cent. quinin. sulph., and 0·8 to 1·0 per cent. cinchonin. sulph.

The variety *Josephiana* of the C. Calisaya, Wedd. (*Hist. Nat. de Quinq. Tab. XXVIII., Fig.* 4) agrees, as far as can - be recognised in young barks, anatomically with the typical form; perhaps the sap fibres are here somewhat more developed.[*]

The red barks (Fig 10 and 13), which grow in the middle region of the district of the Cinchona, with respect to the size of the bast cells, are closely allied to this Calisaya; the lighter coloured sort, very well represented by Delondre and Bonchardat as Quinquina rouge pale (*Quinologie pl.* 8), is also in some degree allied to the Calisaya through the bark formation, truly somewhat less perfect. The sap fibres con-

---

[*] Ruiz, in his *Quinologie*, p. 66, expresses the opinion that his *C. glabra* (*C Lanceolata fl. per.*) gives the calisaya-bark, but revokes it in the *Suplemento*, p. 73 and 97, when he says that the similar yellow colour and the thick bark deceived him, and that in fact both kinds are specifically different. The anatomical structure of a bark in the collection of Pavon, gathered by Tafalla, near Chicoplaya, as a species very like the *C. Lanceolata*, proves the difference of the two barks, although they are outwardly very similar. It is not improbable that this is the bark which was formerly in trade as a light or brown Huamalies-kind of Quina Regia, of which v. Bergen says (*Monographie der Chinarinden*, p. 253), that in form and colour it is not to be distinguished from the genuine, but that it is 25 per cent. less medicinal value. The morphological relations of the C. lanceolata, however, allow us to suppose, as Ruiz also states, that the bark of the same belongs to the medicinally effective sorts.

tinue their functions for the same length of time (Fig. 13).*
The second dark coloured cork covered red bark (Berg's
Quina rubra suberosa, who calls the first species Quina
rubra dura), excellently represented by Delondre and Bonchardat as Quinquina rouge vif. (l. c. pl. 7), of the C. purpurea, micrantha, corymbosa, hirsuta, and others allied by
this cork crust, resemble the above light kind in the order
and size of the bast-cells; the parenchyma cells, which are
between the bast-cells next to the cylindrical, are in this
red bark particularly wide, tangentially extended, and
irregularly divided (Fig. 10), and its sap fibres very soon
alter their functions, as in the *C. Lancifolia* and *Condaminea*,
since in rather older barks they are no longer perceptible.
Weddell now, with Howard (*Pharmaceutical Journal*, 1857)
considers his *variety Erythroderma* of the *C. Ovata fl. per.*
as the mother plant of the red bark. The *C. Ovata* is, however, a large, coriaceous dimple-less leaved species, growing
in the warmer climates, which in New Granada yields no
useful bark, and according to Weddell's opinion is an almost
ineffective bark, exported from Peru and Bolivia as *Jaën
palida*, and it is not improbable that a variety of this species
in Bolivia may bring forth the bark richest in quinine. At
all events the *Erythroderma* of Weddell, if it produces one
of the medicinally valuable red barks, is no variety of the
Ovata, but of a very different species, which a close analysis
of the fruit and blossom will prove, and which Weddell did
not possess.

The grey bark of the *C. Corymbosa m. (Fig. 12)* belongs
to those which have bast bunches in the inner bark of their
youngest parts, and which appear still larger in the older

---

* The bark of the C. nitida fl. per., which Weddell, in his Quinologie,
p. 17, takes for the red bark of trade, and which I examined in the original
specimens of Pavon, who states that it is called Huanuco in trade, is not only
much lighter than this rouge-pale, and has the younger branches covered with a
grey strongly intersected cork-layer like a Loxa bark; but it also contains in
the outer bark next the sap fibres many thick-walled resin-cells, and is, if we
may be guided by the quantity of lime salt, a bark poor in organic bases, and
well deserves Pavon's designation " Huanuco."

parts; it is short fibred in the fracture, since the bunches are placed in a vertical direction and not greatly expanded.

This is also the case in the *C. Stupea*, Pav. (*Quinquina de Loxa rouge fibreuse du Roi d'Espagne*, Guibourt, *Hist. des Drogues iii.* 158), as well as the *C. Chahuarguera*, Pav., *amarilla fina del rey* and *colorada fina del rey* of trade, (*Quinquina Huamalies ferrugineuse*, Guibourt,) whose thin barks covered with a blackish, closely cross-cracked layer of cork, pass for Loxa bark, if under the cork layer, a bark-tissue filled with resinous sap shows itself by a dark shining line on the surface of the fracture of the dried bark. A very similar bark is likewise yielded by the *C. Macrocalyx* Pav.,* and, with respect to the arrangement of the bast-cells, by the *C. Lucumæfolia*, Pav., which, however, in this as in the very different bark formation approaches more the long fibred varieties of the *C. Lancifolia, Obtusifolia*, and the red Cusco bark (entirely agreeing with the *C. purpurea* fl. per. from which Howard derives it).† Weddell considers all these sorts of plants as varieties of the *C. Condaminea*, Hmb. ; against which, however, not only the morphological characters, but the anatomical relations declare ; since the bark of the *C. Condaminea*, according to Humboldt the true *Uritusinga*, deviates by its very thin bast-cells placed in

---

* The *C. Macrocalyx*, Pav. and *C. Chahuarguera*, Pav. are two grey barks, easily recognisable by the bast-cells regularly united in bunches, frequently appearing among the Loxa barks in trade. On account of the inconstancy of the resin-rings, and with the absence of these the tendency to the formation of cork, they are also partly termed Huamalis in trade, whereas that covered with grey cracked peridermis generally has within this a parenchyma filled with resinous sap, and therefore produces the real Loxa. The specimens gathered by Pavon of both kinds are otherwise so similar that one might believe they were at least varieties, if not the same species; in both thickened resin cells appear in the bark tissue filled with dark fluid, according to the development of the peridermis more or less frequent, and the sap-vessels disappear already in very young barks. The bast-cells by the frequently rather larger lumen indicate a less valuable bark. The bast is coarse-splintered in the cross-fracture, in the Chahuarguera less long-splintered than in the C. macrocalyx.

† According to Weddell the bark of the C, micrantha fl. per. (C. scrobiculata Hmb.), Cascarilla roja de Cusco, is called in Peru brown Cusco-bark ; this species, as we know from Poëppig, yields several different kinds of bark, partly known in trade as Huanuco. The young barks of the C. micrantha and purpurea can be distinguished from the first by the sap-vessels, which are well preserved so long ; whilst the barks of the C. purpurea never have sap fibres.

rows, from the former species with its thicker bast cells. Probably all these forms, stated by Weddell as varieties of the C. Condaminea, are more allied to each other than to the *C. Condamine*, Humboldt.

The bark of the *C. Suberosa*, Pav. (*foliis lanceolatis, glandulosis* (scrobiculatis ? K.) *petiolo nervoque centrali sanguineis, Tafalla*) *Quinquina blanc de Loxa, Guib. Corky pale bark*, Howard, is in many respects very similar to the C. corymbosa. The bast-cells stand in radiated rows, single, or joined in bunches in a vertical position, wherefore the fracture is more long-fibred. There are no sap-vessels in the brown horizontally extended bark tissue; under the periderm layer are single groups of thickened resin cells; the grey cracked peridermis is from 1 to 2 lines thick in the bark, beset with numerous small cork warts. The bast-cells are indeed rather thick, but the relatively large lumen indicates an inferior value of the bark; they are sometimes found in concentrical circles.

As to the barks gathered in the proper home of the Cinchona, in north Peru and in southern Ecuador, in the vicinity of Loxa, we have very little information, although la Condamine and Humboldt point to the *C. Condaminea* as the mother plant of an excellent Loxa quina, and Poeppig discovered in the *C. Glandulifera* and *Micrantha* the mother plants of the bark named Huanuco in trade; yet the many different barks which appear in trade under the names Loxa and Huanuco, have not become known; as also those in German trade known as Huamalies, Pseudo-Loxa, Jaën, &c., are uncertain objects in a scientific point of view.

Poëppig fortunately brought with him the barks peeled by him of the *C. Micrantha*, R. et. Pav., and *C. Glandulifera*, *R. et Pav.*, which appear in trade under the names Loxa and Huanuco, so that these could be known and determined. Both species, according to Poëppig, give several varieties of bark, according to the situation of the plant. The barks of the *C. Micrantha** are distinguished outwardly from those of

---

* The barks of the *C. decurrentifolia*, Pav., Casc. crespilla ahumada de Loxa seem almost identical with those of the C. micrantha.

the *Glandulifera* by the whitish colour of the cork-layer, which is split by fine transverse cracks far apart, and long striped excrescences and warts rising on it, and giving it an uneven rough appearance, wherefore it would pass in trade as Huamalies, were not a dark line generally visible on the fracture under the cork layer, a sign of the thick-walled cells filled with resinous sap, which are found in great numbers together in these parts. The fracture of the outer bark is corky and even; that of the cinnamon-coloured inner bark coarse-splintered, indicating the bast cells, which in the older bast are joined into small bunches and are placed vertically; the sap-fibres here soon wither, and in the older barks are no longer perceptible. Delondre and Bonchardat's representations of the Ch. Huanuco, pl. 5, are very like the less corky barks of the micrantha : these chemists obtained from it 0·2 per cent. quinin. sulph. and 0·8 to 0·0 per cent. cinchonin. sulph.

The bark of the *C. Glandulifera* was brought by Poëppig *Pharmazeutisches Centralblatt*, 1835) in two varieties; the better one named cascarilla negrilla, with orange-coloured to a red brown inner bark; the inferior, cascarilla provinciana negrilla, of a lighter cinnamon brown bark; both outwardly alike, covered with a rough cross-cracked dark grey cork, under it a dark shining layer, in the fracture the so-called resin-ring distinctly perceptible; both which peculiarities, in union with the long-splintered bark, procured it in German trade the name of Loxa-bark. According to Reichel (l. c. p. 712) the darker barks agreed closely with the finest Loxa barks of the Bergen collection, whilst the lighter kind, casc. prov. negrilla, seemed identical with the finer (thinner?) sorts of the Bergen Huanuco. The barks of the *C. Glandulifera* are anatomically easy to recognize, from the great number of considerably wider sap-vessels, (the barks gathered by Poëppig near Cuchero, and by Tafalla near Chicoplaya, in the collection of Pavon, agree in the existence of these organs,) as well as from the great number of thick-walled horizontally extended resin-cells, underneath the cork-layer. The tolerably thick bast-cells are very porously thickened, and even in the youngest layers stand several close together, also forming longer vertical bunches, whence the long-splintered fracture of this bark.

Both these, like most of the Loxa barks, are very easy to distinguish from the Uritusinga the real Loxa or *crown quina*, with the microscope, as none of the barks in the Pavon collection, examined by me, have such regularly arranged, relatively thin and uniform bast-cells as this Uritusinga : with the good yellow and red barks there is no mistake possible.

The *C. Nitida fl. per.* is also conjectured by Poëppig to belong to the finest Loxa barks, as well as positively named by Pavon as the bark which appears in trade under the name of Huanuco ; Howard likewise considers the pieces of the Huanuco drawn in *Bergen's Tab. II., Figs. 6 and 12,* as belonging to this species. The barks of the *C. Nitida* of Pavon's collection are, in fact, so like the dark barks of the *C. Glandulifera,* called *Cascarilla negrilla,* that it is difficult to distinguish them in small specimens, if not from the somewhat darker colour of the first. There is a slight anatomical difference in the shorter bast cells of the *C. Nitida,* and the, perhaps, rather early cessation of the functions of the sap-fibres of the bark tissue very rich in resin. The fracture of the bast-layer is short-splintered.

The grey bark of the little systematically known *C. Heterophylla* of Pavon (*Cascarilla nigra foliis scrobiculatis, Pav.*) may also pass for Huanuco, on account of the resin-rings under the dark brown, coarsely cracked cork-layer, with its whitish covering, and fine short-splintered fracture. The rather thick, equal, and perfectly thickened bast-cells give evidence of a medicinally effective bark ; they stand partly single, partly in small groups not connected in a vertical direction. No sap-vessels are found in the dark coloured transversely extended bark-parenchyma ; thickened resin-cells stand single, the dark resin-ring under the cork-layer is brought out by the bark cells filled with dark resinous fluid. It is the bark allied on one hand to the *C. Hirsuta,* Pav., and on the other more to the *C. Corymbosa.*

An outwardly apparent genuine Loxa bark, with dark, grey, long- and ring-shaped cross-cracked peridermis, reddish parenchyma, and long-splintered fracture, is yielded by the likewise systematically unknown *C. Conglomerata*, Pav., *Cascarilla colorada de Jaën de Loxa*, which Pavon calls "very excellent." The bast cells in size and order recall the *C. Micrantha* (*Tab. II., Fig. 14 and* 15); cross-extended, thick-walled resin-cells are found in great number in the dark-coloured bark-tissue; the sap-fibres obliterate early, in older barks are scarcely perceptible.

The bark extraordinarily like the *C. Glandulifera* is that of the *C. Umbellifera, Pav.*,* *Casc. crespilla de Jaën*, especially in the anatomical structure, and also that of the *C. Parabolica*, Ruiz (*Cascarilla con hojas rugosas de Loxa*), *Quinquina payama de Loxa, Guibourt, Hist. de Drogues, III., p.* 159, like the Huanuco in the grey or whitish cork layer, split by deep ring-shaped rather distant cross-cracks, and irregular lighter long ones, but having no resin-ring under it. The grey-yellow bast is long-fibred, and the sap-fibres are still perceptible in tolerably thick barks.

If the grey barks of Loxa be divided into two groups, according to the appearance or absence of the layer of resin-cells of the outer bark, the Loxa and Huanuco will belong to the first, whilst those known as *Huamalies, Pseudo-Loxa,* or *Jaën nigricans* do not possess the so-called resin-ring; to the last belong the Jaën pallida, rubiginosa, Cusco, quina de Maracaibo, &c. On account of their very inconsiderable contents in organic bases they scarcely deserve mention with the above-named medicinally effective barks; they are partly imperfectly characterized drugs, belonging to similar or different species, the derivation of which is not yet known with certainty.

The *Loxa, Pseudo-Loxa, Huanuco Jaën pallida*, appear only in quills, probably because the older barks pass in trade as *Huamalies, rubiginosa, &c.* The *Ch. de Maracaibo* has already

---

* Of this species of Pavon, not yet described, the original specimens indeed exist in the Berlin Royal Herbarium ; but, as Dr. Klotzsch was examining them, they were inaccessible to me.

been mentioned, it is probably no longer in trade; by Huamalies is understood the brown or grey barks, with corky surface on which warts have grown, probably of the *C. Hirsuta*, R. et Pav., and of other species, whilst the Pseudo-Loxa brown or dark cinnamon-coloured bark, with a grey and very cracked almost scaly surface like the Loxa, and the Jaën pallida, the light, long-wrinkled, rather smooth barks, with fine and few transverse cracks, are probably derived from the *C. ovata fl. per.* Of the Ch. Cusco, Delondre and Bonchardat distinguish a brown, yellow, and red variety ; the latter is a bark similar to the Ch. flava fibrosa in the fracture, but of a brown-red, in size and order of the bast cells like the Uritusinga, and seems to bear the same relation to this, as the reddish variety of the flava fibrosa to the flava dura; all are extremely poor in organic bases, particularly in quinine, therefore not of any immediate interest medicinally.

The brown Cusco bark (*Delondre, Tab.* 19), according to Weddell, is derived from the *C. Scrobiculata*, Hmb. (identical with the *C. Micrantha fl. per.*), which partially appeared in trade as Huanuco. The red Cusco (*Delondre, pl.* 3), according to Howard, is from the *C. Purpurea fl. per.*

Delondre and Bonchardat describe, under the name *Caravoya*, another brown-yellow bark like the Huamalies in the corky surface, but with a resin-ring, and in some degree with the whitish coarsely intersected peridermis of the Huaunco, and smooth short-fibred fracture, which come, from the province of the same name, by way of Arica or Arequipa to Europe, and from which they obtained 1·5 to 1·8 per cent. quinin. sulph., and 0·4 to 0·5 cinchon. sulph. This bark does not appear to be the same as that described by Weddell under the same name, Hist. Nat. des Quinq., p. 61, whose scales, as in the Calisaya, are said to come off, leaving trough-shaped indentations ; for it is besides most improbable that the large leathery dimpleless leaved *C. Ovata fl. per.* should give a good fever bark. Ruiz also (Quinologia, p. 74) states that the bark of the *C. Ovata* is of no value in trade, and that it can be used only as an astringent tonic external remedy.

The *Jaën pallida*, Weddell derives from the *C. Ovata, R. et
Pav.*, and it certainly agrees with the barks appearing under
this name, as well with those gathered by Pavon, as with the
barks of this species examined by me. Under the yellow-grey
long-wrinkled and fine cross-cracked cork-tissue there are
found thickened resin-cells in the outer bark, without, however, forming a connected layer. In the cinnamon-coloured
parenchyma there are wide sap-fibres, often filled with en-
dogene cells, and in the inner bark bast cells are found
placed in rows, or joined in radiated bunches, or also standing
single, of smaller diameter, like those of the Uritusinga,
wherefore the fracture is long-splintered. It is an almost
valueless bark, and may be held in equal estimation with the
Maracaibo and Tucuyensis bark, perhaps somewhat richer in
organic bases than the barks of the pubescens, Vahl, and cordifolia, Mut., which belong to the completely useless sorts,
and rank with the Ladenbergia.

The *Casc. amarilla fina de Hinta*, the *C. lutea of Pavon*,
is in every respect similar to the *C. Ovata;* the bast
cells being somewhat thicker. The systematic place of the
C. Lutea of Pavon is little known, as the analysis has
shown that it really deserves the appellation of *fina ;* in this
respect Pavon's statements are not to be relied on, as his
C. Dichotoma teaches us. On the whole I have made use of
Pavon's bark collection with great caution ;[*] and the barks of
Pavon, here cited in comparisons, I am convinced require
another investigation in their native places.

CONCLUSION.

As a result of the investigation of the medicinal quina
barks, a certain analogy was presented in the contents in
organic bases with the form of the bast cells, as the thickest

---

[*] I have to thank Professor Mitscherlich, director of the Pharmacological
collection in Berlin, for the use of the same, for the purpose of this investigation.

and most perfectly thickened bast cells were found in the red and yellow barks, the Quina barks richest in organic bases. This is proved for the different varieties of the *C. Lancifolia,* also for the different species of Cinchona in general.

The difference of climate, in which each kind or species grows, has the greatest influence on the contents in organic bases,[*] although it is most probable that each morphologically different form gives an average content in organic bases.

The bast-cells are not the holders of the organic bases, but most probably the not woody tissue of the inner bark; single cells of this are sometimes found filled with grains of oxalate of lime, particularly abundant in the barks of the Cinchona and Ladenbergia poor in organic bases.

The sap-fibres disappear early in those barks rich in organic bases, whilst in those of the Ladenbergia, and in the soft-leaved Cinchona, they often remain long active.

---

[*] It is not discovered whether the alteration in the constitution of one and the same form of plant, caused by the climate, always corresponds with the size of the bast-cells. My barks of the *C. Corymbosa,* collected for this purpose, have unfortunately been lost through the negligence of the agent in Barbacoas, J. A. Rincon, who left the chest of natural history collections, which contained this bark, stored a year in Tumaco, where they were then said to have been burnt.

NOTES ON THE CINCHONA TREES OF HUANUCO,

(IN NORTHERN PERU,)

Translated from p. 217–23, and p. 257–64 of Vol. II., of
" Reise in Peru, während der jahre 1827–32,"

VON EDUARD POËPPIG,

Professor an der Universität zu Leipzig.

The collection of the fever bark (*Cascarilla*), and the trade in it, is the especial cause of the colonization of the wild mountains of Chinchao and Cuchero, in the province of Huanuco. The introduction of this very profitable trade dates from about 1785; for, in spite of the very high price obtained for the barks in Loxa, during many years no one thought of making use of the known kinds of quina of Huanuco, for an equally profitable business. A short time after the opening of this trade, the speculators (some very active old Spanish colonists, especially Biscayans) had become so rich that they found successors from all sides who, not possessing landed property, were inclined to undertake distant expeditions, partly in the wild forests beyond the river, in the dominion of the independent Indians; partly in the damp hot forests of the lower missions (Chicoplaya and Pampa hermosa), collecting an inferior, but certainly an easily accessible bark. These poor and less scrupulous speculators were guilty of many deceptions and adulterations, and furnished bad goods; for the preservation of the trade was of less importance to them, than to the real proprietors of the large cinchona forests of Cuchero, Pillao, and Cassapi. Various fever barks came into trade from the provinces north of Huanuco, under the name of genuine Huanuco barks, and hence it occurred that these were soon distrusted in Europe, or declared to be only of medium quality. They, however by no means deserve this reputation, since it is proved from the barks gathered and compared by me, that they are to be numbered among the best sorts. At the outbreak of the revolution, partly from want of capital, partly from the emigration of the real speculators in this trade, and as the intercourse was for a long time interrupted, and no new trade had taken the place of that with Cadiz, and the few foreign merchants of Lima, from their want of knowledge of the bark trade, at that time declined any large purchase; the goods at first accumulated in Huanuco, then important losses occurred, and the old and experienced bark collectors (*Cascarilleros*) dispersed from want of work, so that since 1815 no one has carried on this business. The present possessors of Cassapi, Cuchero, and Pampayaco have often endeavoured to restore this trade, which offers them extraordinary advantages, for after a rest of fifteen years the trees have grown up again so high, that they thought in the first year to be able with little trouble to gather 12,000 arrobas (in value about 60,000 dollars). During the war the bark of the *Yungas* or temperate mountain forests of La Paz, and other districts of Bolivia, called *Calisaya* in trade, found a passage to Europe by way of Arica. Perhaps the employment of foreign capital in the contracts with the bark collectors there, rather than the reported great superiority of the bark itself, is the cause that the merchants of Lima, on whom many houses in Arica depend as customers, strongly support the *Calisaya* trade, whilst they decline any connection with Huanuco. It is at present impossible to obtain exact information as to the number of *arrobas** of Huanuco bark, which in better times used to go to Lima, as the trade was partly in the hands of the lesser speculators, and carried on without any connection with the larger bark merchants in Huanuco. Old inhabitants of this town, who owed their property to the bark trade, believed that about 24,000 *arrobas* (of 25 Spanish pounds) had been exported from the whole province in the best years, and the very estimable Don Jose Espinosa, once occupying the first position in this trade, added that the

---

* Arroba = 25 lbs.

speculators without property who wandered about in the wilderness, only in a few cases obtained more than three or four hundred *arrobas*, whilst the great haciendas, who naturally permitted no strangers to fell and peel the cinchona trees in their forests, gathered from two to three thousand *arrobas*, according to the size of the district. Cuchero* possesses the greatest riches, in these trees, and therefore one of its earliest possessors, D. José Bidurrezaga, succeeded in a few years in obtaining, from his forests, about 6,000 *arrobas*, according to the usual prices of bark, at that time producing an income of more than 90,000 dollars. At present this trade in the province of Huanuco may be considered extinguished, and 50 *arrobas* can scarcely find their way to Lima, in small parcels. They are there mixed with the inferior sorts of Bolivia, or used as a means of improving the finer sorts of Truxillo bark, which likewise appear in trade only in very small quantities, and thus belong to the worst kinds known. In the large haciendas, where it was easy to obtain exact local knowledge, the search for the fever barks was conducted with regularity, by dividing the whole forest into parts. Distant expeditions were not undertaken, since the labourers always kept the dwellings of the hacienda near enough to be able to return to them in a few hours, and the whole business was only occasionally engaged in. It was, however, quite different when the speculator without property instituted the search for barks in the high mountains beyond the river Huallaga, and at the sources of the Talumayo. In the vicinity of the *Cinchona* districts there always dwelt labourers, who, much too proud for common agriculture, procured themselves a higher rank as *Cascarilleros* or bark-collectors, and, although mostly people of colour, expected more consideration than the common day labourer (*Peon*), and made their conditions for an expedition with the speculator, according to their inclinations. A contract was generally made, according to a system equally disadvantageous to both parties, and only to be explained by the scanty population. The *Cascarillero*

* Called by Pritchett *Cocheros*.

obtained a credit of from 60 to 100 dollars, which he took in brandy and silver money for gambling, seldom in useful articles. It was necessary to furnish him with food of the best kind, and tools, at the expense of the speculator. The whole company, consisting of ten or more men, then set out, well armed, for the wilderness, and penetrated on foot, and combating great obstacles, as far as the regions where no one could claim the soil as their property, and where numerous bark trees existed. There they erected some very simple forest huts, established themselves as comfortably as possible, and soon began their business; but, besides the proper *Cascarilleros*, they employed a number of common day labourers, partly to smooth the rough roads on the extraordinarily steep mountains, over which the bark was carried out of the wilderness, and partly to procure food from time to time. Not content with the stems growing singly, which in fact would not have been sufficient to cover the expenses, the *Cascarilleros* sought the clumps (*manchas*) in which the *Cinchonas* are found growing together. For this purpose a high rocky point or projecting tree was climbed; experience and sharp sight soon discovered these clumps by their dark colour, and the peculiar reflection of light of the leaves, easily observable on sunny days at a distance, even in the midst of these endless expanses of forest. The Indian, with never erring instinct, was then the leader of the whites, for he conducted them for hours through the forest to the *Cinchonas*, although the forest knife was obliged to be used at every step. When one part of the tree was stripped of its bark, (a single considerable clump, under favourable circumstances, gave 50 *arrobas*), this was packed, in its wet condition, in parcels of the weight of three arrobas, and the Indians were loaded with them, and, in spite of the burden and the trackless mountain wilderness, they reached the nearest inhabited place in a relatively short space of time. There the actual speculator awaited them, in order personally to superintend the important business of drying, which would be impossible within the shady forest. All depends on the success here; for the bark easily becomes mouldy and loses its colour, and no art can so far improve its appearance as to conceal from the experienced buyer that it has been spoiled. For every *arroba* of the green bark (*mato*) delivered, the speculator reckoned two reals to the *Cascarillero;* since in good *manchas* an industrious labourer could easily strip from ten to twelve *arrobas* in one day, and the gain to him amounted to above two dollars. If the speculator was obliged to possess a considerable capital, the profit also was very certain and large; for it was calculated that the *arroba* of good bark, the freight to Huanuco included, cost at most seven dollars, even when it was collected at great distances, and in the wildest mountains, and the transport on the backs of Indians had greatly increased the expenses. To the possessor of Cassapi and Cuchero, who had the bark collected near his dwelling, and could load it on mules, the *arroba* cost from three to four dollars, whilst the price of good Huanuco bark in Lima was always from 16 to 20 dollars. Although experience has proved that, at present, scarcely more than 12 dollars would be obtained in Huanuco, yet the expenses are so diminished by the reduction in the price of all implements, and the increase of the demand for labour, that the speculator would still obtain a large profit. The value of the goods always varied in Lima, and even in the most recent times it has been subject to unexpected variations; yet the speculator suffered little from such causes, for he generally furnished by contract. The merchant in Lima could be exposed to no real loss by the fall of a few dollars in the price, for even at the lowest rate a clear gain of several dollars would remain for every *arroba.* Only at great distances from the place of production, and to the ignorant speculators who allowed themselves to be deceived by bad goods from the warmer valleys, could the bark trade be dangerous; and, even in recent times this alone has caused serious loss. The trade with Huanuco bark would undoubtedly be to the advantage of that province, if it could be reckoned upon for a constant supply for the markets, and if the Government, by legal preventive measures, which have often been proposed, and seem to have existed in Loxa a hundred years ago, would put a stop to the adulterations by small collectors. With a little prudence on the part of the Cascarilleros, the various Cinchona trees would never be extirpated, as many persons from a want of knowledge of their peculiarities, have feared.* It is only necessary to observe the precaution of hewing the stem as near as possible to the root, in order to be sure of its after growth. In the milder regions, near Cuchero, this takes place so fast, that after six years the young stems may already be felled again : in the cold region of the forests, in the vicinity of the *Puna* (or alpine table lands), where the most effective *Cinchonas* are found, 20 years are required. The Peruvian, subject to the endemic tertian-ague, has a great prejudice against the use of bark ; for although at present every one knows of its employment in medicine in Europe, and even the Indians share this knowledge, which in the time of Condamine the whites even in Quito did not possess; yet the native believes that the climate of the cold north alone permits the use of the fever-bark. He includes it in the large class of remedies, declared very heating (*muy*

---

* Ulloa, *Notic. Secret.* p. 572, believed in the speedy extirpation of the Cinchona, and proposed legal measures to prevent this evil. Condamine, *Mém. sur l'Arbre du Quinquine* (in *Mém. de l'Acad. Roy. des Sciences*, 1738, p. 226–243), shares in this view, and perhaps with justice, for about Loxa they appear to have pursued quite a different plan in the stripping of the bark, to that in use in the province of Huanuco. The tree is not felled, but is left standing, deprived of its bark. In all these cases, the trees in the tropical forests are attacked by rot with extraordinary rapidity, and hosts of insects, penetrate the stem to complete the work of destruction, and the healthy root becomes infected. The vitality of most of the tropical trees is so great that if all these causes be not united to promote their destruction they will, by the rapidity of the after-growth, overcome the already commenced rot, and throw out the diseased parts, as completely as the animal body accomplishes the healing of large wounds by a similar process. Were not the vegetation stronger in those regions than in the north, the trees must soon succumb to the disproportionately greater influence of decay. The burned down forest, whose ground has been so heated that for the first few days it is scarcely possible to walk over it, in spite of the heat it has suffered, which has calcined the stones on the surface, grows up again from the roots, although in a changed form. Many half burned stems, to the astonishment of the beholders, shoot out again, and even much more delicate plants, which one would have supposed had been transformed into ashes, being on the surface of the ground and exposed to the full glow, recover. Such are the broad-leaved *orchidæ* of the rocky forests, but most particularly a beautiful *Maxillaria* (*M. bicolor, R. Pav.*), whose angular bulbs may properly be regarded as a peculiar stalk formation, growing pressed together on the ground in great numbers, like mosaic, occurring frequently in Pampayaco, and never succumbing to the forest conflagrations.

calientes), and remains firm to an ancient opinion, probably descending from the Arabian doctors, on the properties of food, drink, and medicine, which is found spread over Spain and Portugal, as well as in the colonies of both countries in America.* A bark cannot be approved as a remedy in complaints, whose cause is sought according to an equally old and extended Pathology, in "Inflammation of the blood;" and in a climate where the native, when unwell, thinks he must, above all things, cool or thin (*disalterarse*) his coagulated juices. Truly, from the imprudent use of the bark, much stronger in Peru, all the evil was seen to arise which was developed in Europe from the same cause, and the mischief was ascribed not to quackery, but to the bark itself. Attacked with violent tertian-ague, and without any medicine, in Pampayaco, I made use of the green bark direct from the tree, which I peeled from one growing a few hundred steps distant, and although, in consequence of unavoidable exposure in the rainy season, and the very great exhaustion after eight months wild forest life, the disease returned on three occasions, it was each time conquered within a week. The very unpleasant additional effect, in this case, of the green bark, likewise remarked by all natives, of producing obstinate obstructions, demands consideration. It might be well obviated by a plentiful addition of Epsom salts to the infusion. After the first dose of this fresh and unadulterated remedy, a sensation of general well-being is felt, and after recovery, on the first excursion, one approaches the healing trees with warm feelings of gratitude, whose beautiful reddish blossoms appear in such quantities in January, that their round crowns can be distinguished at a distance. The botanical and other information connected with the Huanuco barks, will be found below.

* Ulloa, *Relac. Hist.* L. vi. c. 2. § 784, mentions the supposed heating property of the *Cinchona*, Condamine (a. a. O. p. 240) its slight use in the country itself.

The Fever Barks of Cuchero, or Huanuco Barks of Commerce.

The principal districts of the bark collectors are in the so-called *Montaña de Huanuco, i.e.*, the forests, which, beginning from the *Ceja* * of the province of Huamalies, descend to the east, covering the northern part of the province of Huanuco, especially the Quebrada of Chinchao, and the mountains of Muña and Acomayo, filling the valleys of the principal rivers, and on its eastern side again ascending the high mountains of Panataguas, and, beyond these, losing itself in the great primitive forests. Perhaps also these grow in the Pajonales of the upper part of the Pampa del Sacramento, of the Rio Pachitea. The boundary line of the *Cascarilleros* of Huanuco took about the following direction :—From San Rafael (on the road to the Cerro de Pasco) along the *Ceja* of the Sierra, *i.e.*, of the eastern declivity of the Andes from Huanuco, through the province Huamalies, as far as a little north of Rio Monzon, and parallel with it into the valley of the Huallaga; after crossing this, up to the Rio Tulumayo, coming from the east, and along the mountains of Panataguas as far as opposite Pozuzo; and again in a westerly direction to its termination. The whole of this country is extraordinarily intersected with deep valleys and chasms, and on the whole exactly resembles the Quebradas † of Chinchao and Cassapi. The *Cascarilleros* of Huanuco did not collect beyond the limits mentioned, as only the shrubby Cinchona occurs there, at greater elevations, whose bark is indeed effective, but has been found by no means proper for trade. Neither did they go farther north down the Huallaga, as all the barks of those much warmer valleys are known to be bad, are easily distinguishable from the genuine Huanuco barks, and are either quite rejected in Lima, or else bought at the lowest price.

---

* *Ceja*, an eyebrow. It here means the brow, or summit of a mountain range.
† Ravine.

· If some Cinchona trees are less sensitive to an increased
temperature than the majority of the sub-alpine species, and
occasionally descend into the warmer valleys, they then
change their nature, as well as the effectiveness of their bark,
a fact which I had an opportunity of proving in the mission
of Tochache, on the upper Huallaga. Condamine appears
not to have known it, but actually makes the strange assertion, that barks from the warmer regions are the most effective (*Mém. sur le Quinquina*, a. a. 6. p. 228), which a few
pages further on (p. 236) he himself contradicts by the statement that the bark from Jaen de Bracomoros is considered
so bad, that it is enough to know that it comes from Cher-
repe, the usual place for the shipping of the Cascarilla de
Jaën, to render it unsaleable in Panama. The environs of
Jaën are very low (200 to 300 T. according to Humboldt;
medium temperature probably the same as the districts of
the lower Huallaga, lying on the same level $= 26°$ C.*),
and produce, even at the present day, a sort of little value,
which is exported as little as the bark of Moyobamba,
Chachapoyas, and Llamas, because in Peru the warm
climate of all those regions of the *Cascarilla* was always
considered unfavourable. The small quantities of bark
exported from Truxillo, the natural harbour of the
northern provinces, is gathered on the Jalcas, east of
Chachapoyas. The bark of Moyobamba is very inferior,
and comes from the *Cascarilla boba*, which is little valued
even in Cuchero, is never gathered there, and under the
warmer sky of Maynas, is quite useless. With such bark
was it that the crafty Peruvians deceived the rather hasty
and eager Brazilians, when, after the expulsion of the
Spaniards, they hoped to partake of the fabled treasures of
Peru even in Maynas, and extended their trading expeditions
as far as Yurimaguas and Moyobamba. It was no wonder
that the speculators of Pará (according to Martius, *Reise*,
iii. p. 1178), cursed the Peruvian bark trade, for the goods
which I also found in Pará still unsold, were of the worst
that ever left Peru. In Moyobamba, the ignorance and

---

* $78\frac{1}{2}°$ Fahrenheit.

E.

eagerness of the first Brazilians, who had penetrated so far, is still mocked at, and in Yurimaguas many hundred-weight of equally bad mouldy rind lay about, which a very speculative sub-prefect of the province (Don Damiano Naxar), in the unfulfilled hope of being able to accomplish the deception a second time, caused to be collected and transported by unpaid Indians, with much trouble, to the place of lading in Maynas.

Barks from the district of the upper Huallaga have never found their way down the Marañon to Brazil; for an intercourse between Cuchero and Tabatinga is impossible, and has never existed; and, besides, the bark trade of Huanuco had ceased before the Brazilians had permission to come to Maynas. In the province of Para even the upper commercial ranks had a prejudice against the traffic with fever bark, for they had never seen the better sorts, and would scarcely ever have obtained the same in any quantity as an article of trade, for, naturally enough, all the exportable products of the Montaña of Huanuco would take the way of Lima and Cape Horn, and never the imagined route of the Marañon, to Europe.

In the cinchona forests of Huanuco they were very particular with respect to local differences, for large speculators gathered only the bark growing on steep declivities, or mountain ridges. All stems were rejected, even when they stood in the very promising groups (*Manchas*), if the soil was damp, and the valleys warm and without a current of air. Therefore there was a great difference even in the price of the harvest of a small district, for the higher and colder the situation the more valued was the bark. The chief stations of the collectors were—Huacarachuco, (an isolated but very rich cinchona forest, beyond the above given limits, belonging to the province Conchucos); Patayrondos, near the source of the river of the same name; Monzon; Pantamayo; Cayumba, (a hamlet of a few scattered houses), all in the province of Huamalies; Cuchero and Cassapi (particularly the chain Cassapillo dividing them); the rather cold hamlet Pillao; the mountains of Panatahuas; the mountains between Pampayaco and Pillao, particularly Lanzabamba,

Marco, Yguacará; Panao with Muña, places whence very fine barks came; Pozuzo, which however furnished only few and inferior barks; and San Rafael, where a small quantity of the finest of all the known barks, the *Cascarilla Hoja de Oliva*, was gathered. With the exception of a few haciendas, the greater part of these lands, rich in cinchona trees, belonged to the king of Spain, or rather to no one, since the wilderness beyond the Huallaga, in particular, was uninhabited, and protected by no forts, nor claimed in any other way by the Government. Every one was allowed to gather, and no single regulation (*Cedula real*) in reference to the cascarilla seems to exist.

The preparations for an expedition were made in April; in May the labourers set out for the forest; and the last bales of green bark arrived in November. The tree was felled close to the root, but all young looking stems (*palos verdes*) were spared, because no profit was to be drawn from them before maturity. The next business was the dividing of the stem (*trozar*) into pieces of one *vara** long; the thinnest boughs only were thrown away The bark is slit lengthways, with knives made on purpose, but some practice is necessary in order not to injure the wood, and to avoid the simultaneous withdrawal of the fibres attached to, and injuring, the bark. By means of this same knife the strips (*lonjas*) of bark are pulled off, as broad as possible, but this must not be done till three or four days after the felling of the trees; for before the moisture between the bark and stem is somewhat dried, it is impossible to peel off those large pieces unbroken, which increase the value of the goods. It is still worse, when by a too hasty peeling of the bark, the thin, whitish-grey, or blackish epidermis, loaded with many *cryptogamia*, falls off, and the separate pieces then appear outwardly smooth and cinnamon-coloured, which makes a great difference in trade, as the English most especially were always of opinion, that a bark was the more powerful, the thicker the epidermis is covered with lichen, &c. On the quick drying of the barks depended the price which they obtained in trade, for in few similar

---

* 100 varas = 110 yards.

articles has prejudice ever been so active as in the *Cinchona*. This is not possible in the thick forests, therefore the packages of fresh bark were sent to the nearest inhabited place, where the speculator of the expedition, or others commissioned by him, receive it. It is laid without any preparation in a very sunny place, and must be guarded with the greatest care from all humidity. A dew for a few hours on the half-dried bark, gives the cinnamon-brown inner part of the fine sorts a blackish appearance, and diminishes the value one half. A sign of the quick drying, consequently of the goodness of the article, is, when the pieces are rolled round in several folds, and present that cylinder without any hollow space (*canutos*), which is seldom found unbroken in Europe. The barks are no less sensitive to atmospheric moisture than the coca *; therefore it is sent as quickly as possible to the warmer climates of the Andes, or to the capital. Some loss is unavoidable; for however quickly the drying may have been managed in the forest region, three or four days after its arrival in Huanuco the article has lost 12 to 15 per cent. in weight. It is packed in bales of four to five *arrobas*, with the greatest care, in order to avoid break-ing the fine rolls, which, in the Montaña,† are two feet long. Generally the packages are bound round with creeping plants (*bejucos, sogas*), and the barks are first sorted in Lima, in order to be packed in chests according to their size and appearance, of different prices, and sent to Europe. The trade with Huanuco bark was very active for about 20 years in Lima, and the article passed in the Spanish markets under the name of *cascarilla roxa*, without being confounded with that called by us *Cortex Chinæ ruber*. The bark, on the other hand, from the neighbourhood of the lower Huallaga, of Huambo, Chachapoyas, &c., was very little esteemed in Cadiz, and called *Cascarilla arollada*. As to the kinds of bark, and the great difference stated to be found in the trees producing them, there existed extraordinary prejudices, not

---

* *Erythoxylon Coca*, a shrub, the leaves of which are chewed by the Peruvian Indians.
† Forest.

only in Europe, but also in Peru, which Condamine remarked (*Journ. du Voy. à l'Equat.* Par. 1751, l. p. 38). Many species were quite rejected; others, without any foundation, considered as particularly fine, and the botanist sees with astonishment how the native, without any visible sign, divides the same species into several different ones, and gives three or more names, according to their products. A single kind (*Cinchona Glandulifera, R., Pav.*), has three names, although scarcely the slightest sign of variation, in a botanical sense, can be discovered. At the same time it was everywhere believed in Peru, that the bark of the stem and of the lower boughs were really effective, and that the thin cylinders (*canutillos*), which were sought for some time in the English trade, were much less fitted for medicinal use. In order to throw some light on the botany of the hitherto so little known Huanuco bark, I have collected and dried the species growing near Pampayaco, in the greatest quantity and perfection, stripped their bark myself, and, after careful drying, sent it to Europe in considerable quantities. I, therefore, now communicate the results of the investigation of the subject obtained in Peru, and what the results of the comparison have been in Europe.

The pharmaceutical barks in the Cinchona districts of Cuchero, are the following :—

1. *Cascarilla negrilla,* comes from the *Cinchona Glandulifera, R., Pav.,* and is considered the finest sort. The tree inhabits only the highest mountains, is more rare than the other species, has a stem from 12 to 15 feet high, on cold mountain tops, becomes even bushy, and gives so little bark that, on an average, only five to six pounds can be expected from one. This bark the Peruvians distinguish by the prevailing blackish epidermis, which now and then only is interrupted in its fresh condition, by very small grey-greenish lichens. The ignorant Indian takes these for integral parts of the bark, and esteems it particularly, if under the larger lichens he discovers a shining black velvet-like substance, in ovals, some lines in size (probably a *Byssus*). The goodness of this bark, according to the assertion of the *Cascarilleros,* is further indicated by a glassy, shining, almost resinous fracture; it is said besides to be on the inner side, the colour

of ripe orange, with slight transitions to bright brown. For the rest, the *canutos* of this sort are always thinner and less woody than in the following. The blossom disperses much fragrance in the forests in February.

2. *Cascarilla provinciana negrilla, C. Glanduliferæ, R., Pav., Varietas.*—Likewise a finer sort, but the product of the same tree, which produces different barks according to its situation. The same species on higher mountains gives the *Cascarilla negrilla*, and in warmer valleys the present kind. The outward appearance is almost the same in both, but the latter is less fiery in colour, and in the inner part more dun or cinnamon-brown. This difference is of no importance, either in European trade, or for medical use.

3. *Cascarilla provinciana, Cinchona Micrantha, R., Pav.* (*variat, α flor. extus roseis, β flor. extus albidis.*)—The tree is of considerable circumference, blossoms in February, and often gives eight to ten *arrobas* of dried bark. This is distinguished from that near Huanuco by its striking whitish colour, and great roughness of surface. It is thicker and more woody, the fracture fibrous, and of a light cinnamon colour. Three sorts are known in trade.

4. *Pata de gallinazo.**—The bark of the younger and upper branches of the preceding species. From a prejudice it was considered by the foreign merchants as a very fine sort, although the Peruvians declared it inferior. Its great thinness and slightly woody texture gave it this unmerited consideration, the difficulty of obtaining it in quantities its high price. The name (*claw of the turkey buzzard, Vultur Anra. L.*) comes from the blackish and radial marks of some species of *Graphis* found upon it. The *Pata de gallireta*, mentioned by Ruiz and Pavon, is the bark of the *Cinchona Ovata, R. Pav. Flor. Peruv.* II. p. 52, not occurring about Cuchero, and different from the present.

5. *Cascarilla hoja de oliva, Cinchona Nitida, R., Pav.?*—The bark exists only in small fractured pieces, and is not gathered. It equals the finest sorts of Loxa barks, surpassing them in resinousness and bitterness. The tree, unknown

---

* Mr. Howard considers this to be a distinct species, and has named it *C. Peruviana.*

to me, grows only in the coldest mountains, has a straight stem scarcely eight feet high, and gives very little bark, which is however so valued that the vice-roys and corregidores sent it as a present only to the king and grandees of Spain. It never appeared in trade. The flowers are of the deepest red, provided in the interior with snow-white wool, and are developed in May. These last circumstances accord with a Cinchona which I found in April 1830 as a very small tree on the Cuesta del Carpis, the *Cinchona Heterophylla, Ruiz.*, a species distinguished by hanging blossoms, which may more probably be considered as a variety of the *C. Pubescens, Vahl.* (De C. Prod. iv. 353).*

---

* Particular attention is directed to this species, and to the following remarks, as it is possible that it may be identical with the species without name, now in charge of Mr. McIvor, on the Neilgherry hills. Mr. Pritchett obtained specimens of this sort, on the Cuesta del Carpis, both of the plant itself and of its bark. (*See* his Report, p. 2.) *C. R. M.*

Mr. Howard sees no reason to doubt the identity of this species, found by Poëppig, with that of Pritchett, and both with *C. Obovata* of Pavon.

Pavon's description is as follows :—

Chinchona Obovata, foliis oppositis, petiolatis, obovatis, pedunculis paniculato corymbosis, terminalibus ; calycibus floribusque rosaceo-rubicundis.

Frutex bi-orgyalis, parum ramosus.

Truncus erectus, cortice cinereo-nigrescente aspero levidoque obductus ; comâ ramosâ.

Rami erecti, teretes, teneri, obtuse tetragoni, pubescentes, apice foliosi, purpurascentes.

Folia opposita, petiolata, obovata, undulata, integerrima, acumine obtuso, marginibus revolutis, supra glabra nitidaque, subtus pubescentia, maxime nervosa venosaque, venis reticulatis, nervo centrali venisque purpurascentibus.

Petioli teretes, superne canaliculati, basi incrassati, rubicundi.

Stipulæ interfoliaceæ, oppositæ, oblongæ, integerrimæ, undulatæ, erectæ, cauli adpressæ, nervo intermedio crasso prominente, obtusæ, deciduæ.

Pedunculi communes terminales, foliosi, oppositi, paniculato-corymbosi.

Foliolis oppositis, petiolatis, ovatis, integerrimis, obtusis.

Pedicelli oppositi, 3–4 flori, bracteolis parvis, ovatis, concavis, acutis, in medio et ad basim singuli florum pedicelli oppositis et solitariis.

Calyx rubicundus.

Corolla rosaceo-rubra, laciniis intus villoso-tomentosis, villis albicantibus. Tubus incurvatus.

Stamina. Filamenta quinque, aliquando sex. *Antheræ* lineares, intra tubi faucem.

Capsula lineari-oblonga, bilocularis, bivalvis, a basi dehiscens.

Semina ut in ceteris speciebus.

Habitat in altis frigidis locis, Carpis nominatis, Chinchao vico silvis.

Floret Julio et Augusto.

Poëppig found the specimens, which Klotzsch of Berlin gave to Mr. Howard,

6. *Cascarilla boba colorada, Cinchona Purpurea, R., Pav.*—
A tree of great height and circumference, which may very
easily be distinguished from all allied *Cinchonæ*, from
its very large membranaceous leaves being covered on
the under side, with strongly projecting violet-red veins,
which, when young, are so numerous that the whole leaf
appears of the same colour. In a fresh condition the bark is
exceedingly bitter, and would, perhaps, be useful in the preparation of cheap decoctions, as it can be sold at very low
prices. It is not collected at all, and served only occasionally
for adulteration, which, however, could be discovered by a
very superficial examination. According to Göbel (*Waaren-
kunde II. p.* 62) the derivation of the *Cascarilla boba* was
hitherto uncertain, as it was attributed now to the *C. Cordifolia, Mut.*, now to the *C. Macrocarpa, Vahl.*

7. *Corteza del Azahar, Cinchona Magnifolia,* * R., Pav.*—A
stately tree, with uncommonly large white blossoms, dispers-
ing the most delicious orange smell. The bark is never

---

on the summit of the Cuesta del Carpis, between Acomayo and Chinchao, in
April 1830. Klotzsch named this species *C. Discolor.* Mr. Howard says that
the bark brought home by Pritchett seems to constitute a variety of *C. Pubescens*, and yields kinovic acid and aricine, which, as sulphate, does not
crystallize, but forms a peculiar trembling jelly. The bark of this species can
never become of any importance in commerce.

Pritchett, as well as Klotzsch, and apparently Poëppig, believe it to be the
species called by Ruiz " *Cascarilla con hojas parecidas a las del oliva,*" which
is valuable.

Mr. Howard hesitates to believe that *C. Obovata* represents the origin of
Cascarilla con hojas del oliva of Ruiz, as the leaves do not resemble those of
the olive, nor does the bark of the latter agree with that brought home by
Pritchett.

This species, the *C. Discolor* of Klotzsch, is given in Weddell's list, as
doubtful, together with one other, the *C. Palalba* of Pavon. Weddell allows
19 true *Cinchonæ*, and these two doubtful; the other plants, which had been
called *Cinchonæ* by other authors, and which are 73 in number, are degraded
by Weddell to other genera of cinchonaceous plants.

Mr. Pritchett's " species without name " may be Poëppig's *C. Purpurea*,
which is quite worthless. Mr. Howard, however, tells me that he does not
think that Pritchett's " species without name," can be the *C. Obovata*,
because he is almost sure that Pritchett had not any capsules of that sort. " It
" is more likely," he says, " the species which, as represented in the specimens
" he gave me, is a sort from Tingo, apparently akin to *C. Nitida*, and having
" all the aspect of a very good bark, as far as I can judge from the leafy branch
" sent."—*C.R.M.*

* These are not *Cinchonæ*, but belong to the allied genus of *Cascarillas.*

termed *Cascarilla*, *i. e.* fever bark in the narrower sense, as the common Indian does not consider the *Azahar* as a *Cinchona*. With the exception of that of the stem, the bark resembles the young oak-bark, is from four to five lines thick, woody, therefore does not roll up into quills; is slightly bitter, never collected for sale, but has been now and then used in pharmacy in Europe, and is employed in small quantities for the purpose of adulteration.*

---

* For the following remarks on the species of the above mentioned barks collected by me, considered as articles of trade in Peru, I have to thank Herr Reichel, Apothecary at Hohenstein in Saxony, who has perhaps brought together one of the largest collections of *Cinchona* in Germany, and obtained the specimens of the large collection of Herr von Bergen in Hamburg :—

" All the barks appeared particularly well preserved at the examination, and in no case rubbed off; they were very numerous and therefore offered a number of very instructive forms; their appearance was uncommonly fresh, and on this account at the first view, on a superficial examination, might deceive in the comparison with the generally much broken and rubbed article of trade.— 1. *Cascarilla negrilla.* Mostly pieces a good foot long, from $\frac{1}{2}$ to $\frac{3}{4}$ of an inch in diameter, quite straight almost throughout, always double rolled; the outer surface very rough, with many cross-furrows running round; the colour varying, slate ash-, even reddish-grey; covered with many white spots and *Cryptogamia*; the under-surface delicate-fibrous, but smooth and cinnamon-coloured ; the bark is hard; the fracture tolerably straight and resinous ; the smell like tan and musty ; the taste acid, astringent, and lastingly bitter. The appearance, as well as the other signs, but especially the comparison with Bergen's original specimen, leave no doubt, that this bark is to be esteemed equal to the finest Loxa-barks. It formerly appeared, but seldom and in inconsiderable pieces, among the barks of Lima. It produced a beautiful, red-yellow`decoction, which, by means of oxide of iron, and a solution of tartar-emetic gave the hope of a very estimable article.—2. *Cascarilla provinciana,* the so-called Huanuco bark of trade, closely agrees with the finer sorts of the same, in Bergen's collection. Mostly pieces of $1\frac{1}{2}$ to 2 feet long, $\frac{3}{4}$ to 1 inch diameter ; all the rolls spirally wound, a general sign, without exception, of the younger Huanuco-barks; bark and splinter closely connected; the exterior thickly covered with white spots and small *Cryptogamia* ; taste at first acid, then strong and lastingly bitter ; the cross slits peculiar to the Huanuco bark were also present here in great quantities. The decoction was of a beautiful red-brown, and acted towards the re-agents named, like that of an inferior Loxa-bark.— 3. *Pata de gallinazo.* Evidently the bark of the youngest branches of No. 2., with which it agrees very much. The pieces at most 1 foot long and $\frac{1}{4}$ inch thick. They form a small portion of the so-called Lima-bark of trade. The decoction gave the same result as in the previous ones.—4. *Cascarilla boba,* the Huamalies bark of trade. Certainly present in great quantity, but mostly consisting only of very young barks in which the wart-like elevations are in part entirely wanting, in place of which, however, they possess the peculiar long wrinkles in so much greater number, and which distinguish the Huamalies

F

The *Cinchona Rosea, R., Pav.*, not rare about Cuchero, appears in the form of a very fine tree, which, in size and the form of the branches, rather resembles the European white beech, is adorned in July with innumerable pale violet flowers, and by its growth, circumference of the stem, and the great hardness of its wood, is distinguished completely from the other *Cinchonæ*, mostly only 6 to 12 inches in the diameter of their stems. Its name, *Palo de San Juan*, indicates its time of blossoming. The bark is not used, for no one believes that the tree belongs to the *Cinchonæ*, whose properties would undoubtedly be found in the thin and smooth bark of the riper boughs. The adulteration of the good sorts with bad, and in part with quite foreign barks, was very common, and the *Azahar* is named, whose bark, however, is too coarse and weighed too heavy, and was distinguishable by its sharp unpleasant bitter taste from the always rather aromatic tasting genuine kind.*

The bark of the *Lucumo*, perhaps of an *Achras* or *Cervantesia*, served for the same purpose, it was, however, too foreign looking to be mixed in large quantities, and that of the *Lluto* (*Clusiæ n. sp.*), a fine tree with large white flowers. Yet several deny that these barks have been thrown among the *Cinchona* barks. Extract was prepared long ago on the spot, and went mostly to Spain, and in Loxa this business was carried on a hundred years ago (1743, *Condamine Voy., &c., I. 186*). After the decline of the bark trade of Huanuco, an English merchant tried to make money by preparing a great quantity of extract in Cuchero, but his

bark from all others. In the younger specimens the colour falls very much into fawn, in the older ones the wart-like elevations appear very much, and the brown spots are more numerous, which, when many older barks lay close together in a small space, gives them a well-known brown colour. All the pieces are covered with many white spots, but perfect lichen is not there, except on a few small specimens of the *Usnea Cinchonarum*. The rolls are $1\frac{1}{2}$ to $2\frac{1}{4}$ feet long, $\frac{1}{4}$ to 1 inch thick; the taste a little acid, and predominantly bitter, but the bitterness appears only after chewing for some time. The decoction, after cooling, was of a yellow clay-colour, and acted, to the re-agents employed, like that of a quina-bark, certainly useful but very inferior."

* Three of the species mentioned by Poëppig are not Cinchonæ at all, but belong to other genera. His *C. Rosea* is *Lasionema Rosea*; *C. Magnifolia* is *Cascarilla Magnifolia*; and *C. Purpurea* is another species of *Cascarilla*. They are of no value.—*C. R. M.*

goods found a bad sale in England, for the Quinine had been already too much imported. The samples brought with him, which were preserved very well for two years in the damp primitive forests by enclosing them in tin cases, were declared excellent by connoisseurs in Germany, and possessed an aroma, which is quite lost in the extract prepared in Europe from the dried bark.

The *cryptogamia*, appearing on the barks of Cuchero, besides many undetermined species are:—1. On the *Cascarilla provinciana: Asterisca cinchonarum. Graphis subcurva, G. byssiseda, Lecanora pallida, pallida-lava, Verrucaria parasema*; of larger lichens only the *Usnea cinchonarum*. 2. On the *Cascarilla negrilla : Lecanora punicea, Lecidea grisea, Verrucarica exasperata, Graphis subbifida, Variolaria mirocephala. Parmelia melanoleuca.*

LONDON:
Printed by GEORGE E. EYRE and WILLIAM SPOTTISWOODE,
Printers to the Queen's most Excellent Majesty.
For Her Majesty's Stationery Office.

CPSIA information can be obtained
at www.ICGtesting.com
Printed in the USA
LVHW030834050420
652274LV00012B/2371